Deliver Us From Eden

A Screenplay

Strake Colton

Copyright © 2020 by Strake Colton

All rights reserved. No part of this publication may be reproduced, distributed or transmitted in any form or by any means, without prior written permission.

Blue Morpho Press New Mexico
3621 Zafarano St., Ste. 218
Santa Fe, New Mexico 87507 USA
bluemorphopress.nm@gmail.com

Publisher's Note: This is a work of fiction. Names, characters, places, and incidents are a product of the author's imagination. Locales and public names are sometimes used for atmospheric purposes. Any resemblance to actual people, living or dead, or to businesses, companies, events, institutions, or locales is completely coincidental.

Cover and book design Laurie McDonald

Deliver Us From Eden/Strake Colton. — 1st ed.
ISBN 978-0-9678995-3-4

And I will put enmity between you and the woman,
And between your seed and her seed;
He shall bruise you on the heel,
And you shall bruise him on the head.
— Genesis 3:15

INTRODUCTION

From Donald Trump and Judge Brett Kavanaugh to Bill O'Reilly and Harvey Weinstein, entitled, narcissistic, hyper-masculine, conservative white American men have never wielded so much power and authority as they have in the first two decades of the third millennium. This masculine power-grab penetrates all aspects of society, and throughout the American South, particularly in Texas, rattlesnake wranglers also embody these negative qualities. The rattlesnake roundup provides the backdrop for narratives of tyranny, misogyny, and the myth of the virile Wild West male, and these explicit connections, combined with masculine domination of a difficult environment, confer a deep significance on these events.

During weekend rattlesnake roundup events, usually held in March as the snakes are waking up from their winter brumation (the extreme slowing down of metabolism), thousands of rattlesnakes are hunted and captured. Men in paramilitary attire, who in everyday life are ranchers and business owners, transform into mythic heroes armed with snake hooks, trash cans, and gas canisters. They collectively storm local snake dens, spraying gas into their hiding places to force the hapless, torpid snakes into the open air. The captured snakes are deposited in holding bins, later to be milked, butchered, skinned, and eaten, and this elaborate ritual is conducted ostensibly to control the species. However, snakes play an important role in the predator/prey hierarchy, and when the snake population is decimated, the rodent population proliferates.

Rattlesnake roundups are distorted in another way. Snakes are considered a deadly threat to local communities; however, statistics show that people are more likely to die from contact with hot tap water, by accidental suffocation in bed, or by a lightning strike than from a snake bite.

Evidence abounds that roundups are more of a psychological than a physical purging, an overt expression of male rage.

Drawing on ancient Hebrew, Hindu, Egyptian, and Assyrian epics, rattlesnake roundups reveal that myth is alive and well in this contemporary, if somewhat bizarre, spring ritual. Customarily, spring represents renewal and regeneration, symbolized in the skin shed by the snake. But rattlesnake roundups are an abortion of spring: The snakes are delivered into the jaws of death while the redbuds begin to blossom and the oak trees unfurl their leaves. Most significant, some roundup participants point to the story of Adam and Eve as "historical" justification for their actions and engage in behaviors usually reserved for nations at war. Roundups are a ritual reinforcement of traditional roles and a murderous paradigm for the superstitious link between snakes, women, and evil.

The ancient Greeks understood the psychological power of snakes, perhaps due in part to the myth of Heracles. One of Heracles's twelve labors was to destroy the nine-headed Hydra and, additionally, the hundred-headed serpentine dragon Ladon, which Heracles succeeded in doing (Hera, Zeus's wife, had trained the Hydra specifically to kill Heracles.) Other serpent elements figure largely in Greek mythology; e.g., Python the Earth dragon, and, of course, Medusa, the snake-headed Gorgon. Informed by their tradition of myth, when going to battle at sea, the Greeks carried huge vessels filled with vipers and when close enough to enemy ships, catapulted the vessels into their ships. The vipers were a powerful distraction, if nothing else. Early settlers of the Western United States also understood the psychological power of snakes, hanging rattlesnake skins and carcasses on barbed wire fences surrounding their property to frighten and deter trespassers.

Perhaps it is more than snakes that roundups purport to control. Typically, roundups are men-only events, and women are allowed to participate only in ways dictated by men. These usually involve activities that reinforce traditional women's roles (the cooking of snakes) or that sanction the objectification of women, as in beauty contests where participants are no older than eighteen. Wanting to please their fathers, brothers, and other important male influences, the contestants all try earnestly to be the perfect woman. The winning girl often must milk a rattlesnake in front of an audience, inserting the young woman directly into the Garden of Eden myth and its snake/woman conflict. And, of course, the act of milking a snake by a girl at the cusp of womanhood is a ritualized initiation into her sexuality, overt in its signifiers. Worthy of note, in some roundups, the night before the activities are to begin, girls and women are not allowed into the areas where the snakes will be collected and killed, and if they appear, they are considered available for sexual exploitation. Like the snakes, the girls are stripped of their power.

Rattlesnake roundups connect to an earlier time in the Wild West when gender roles were explicit and inalienable, when fundamental Christianity was the dominant religion and people of different faiths were demonized, when animals were considered the property of humans, when outsiders were viewed with suspicion and hostility, and when crimes against women weren't considered punishable or even to be bothered with. Perpetuating these same damaging cycles in the third millennium suggests the Nietzschean eternal recurrence, a perpetual turning of the hourglass of existence, and contributes to the many man-made threats to our very survival.

Eva Rome
from *What It Means: Myth, Symbol, and Archetype in the Third Millennium, Vol. 1*

AUTHOR'S NOTE

The first draft of *Deliver Us From Eden* was written over twenty-five years ago. The screenplay was put aside, but with the rise of the #MeToo movement in 2006, and in light of current events, the issues addressed in the screenplay are even more relevant today than they were in the 1990s. *Deliver Us From Eden* explores tyranny, misogyny, incest, and redemption within a traditional story template, that of vengeance of kin against kin (the father/son difficulty) and, as a sub-plot, the obstacles to love.

The unconventional screenplay formatting I've used is intentional.

—Strake Colton

THE MAIN CHARACTERS

Deliver Us From Eden is set in the fictional West Texas town of Eden's Lair.

Corky Dodds	Rattlesnake wrangler and organizer of the Eden's Lair Annual Rattlesnake Roundup.
Valjean Dodds	Corky's son and detractor.
Darlynn Dodds	Corky's daughter and Valjean's sister.
Rose McGrath	An elementary school teacher who's moved to Eden's Lair from Dallas.
Richard McGrath	Rose's husband who stayed behind in Dallas.
Kundoo	An East Indian convenience store manager and mystic.
Chuck	Corky's right-hand man.
Steve	Chuck's sidekick.
Dr. Ennis	The town doctor.
Bob	TV personality and Master of Ceremonies, the Miss Snake Charmer contest.
Ulysses S. Pierce	A greenhorn Texas Ranger.

DELIVER US FROM EDEN

FADE IN:

EXT. THE ESCARPMENT – DAY
A view of Eden's Lair, a desolate West Texas town, from a rocky overlook. Eden's Lair is a small, dusty, homespun place, its focal point a large coliseum.

EXT. HIGHWAY – DAY
A billboard welcomes visitors. "Eden's Lair, Home of the World's Largest Rattlesnake Roundup."

EXT. COLISEUM – DAY
Cars and school buses pull into the parking lot. A loudspeaker blares country and western music. A large papier-mâché rattlesnake, coiled and ready to strike, sits at the entrance to the coliseum under a banner that reads "Git Them Rattlesnakes 4 They Git U."

Two EMTs open the back doors of an ambulance parked near the entrance and remove a gurney.

INT. COLISEUM – DAY
Fourth grade teacher, ROSE McGRATH, a beautiful woman in her late twenties, with blonde hair, luminous skin, and a vulnerable yet determined look in her eyes, enters the coliseum with her class.

Members of an all-male organization known as the JUNIOR SNAKE WRANGLERS (JSWs) hand out miniature baseball bats to the children as they file in. Rose's white, starched, long-sleeved shirt and straight black skirt look prim compared to the dusty blue jeans and western shirts worn by the Junior Snake Wranglers.

The snake pit, an octagon of plywood walls. Standing in the center of the pit, CORKY DODDS, a weathered snake wrangler in his early fifties, flips the lid on a wooden box and yanks three large rattlers out with his snake hook, dropping them on a circular table. Corky wears a western shirt with his name embroidered on the back, a rattlesnake head bolo tie, and a head-worn microphone.

Rose and the children take their seats on the bleachers. Everyone's eyes are riveted to the sinister shapes undulating on the table.

A JSW dressed as a CLOWN blows up several large balloons with helium and hands them to Corky's son VALJEAN, an impossibly handsome blue-eyed, light brown-haired man in his mid-twenties. Valjean stands near the table holding the bunch of balloons and a snake hook.

Rose and Valjean steal glances at each other; they lock eyes and smile. His face reddens, embarrassed by the task he's been relegated to, and she lowers her eyes, trying to stifle her widening smile. Valjean keeps the snakes on the table with his snake hook while Rose keeps her fourth graders in line.

> CORKY: Well awright! Welcome to the kids-only preview of the 25th Annual Eden's Lair, Texas, Rattlesnake Roundup. A special welcome to Eden's Lair Elementary and their newfangled fourth-grade teacher, all the way from Dallas, Miss Rose McGrath.

The children applaud politely. The attention embarrasses Rose, but she smiles graciously.

> CORKY: My name is . . . ya'll know my name, don't cha? I started this dang thing, didn't I? What's my name?

> CHILDREN (tentatively): Corky.

> CORKY: What? I can't hear you.

> CHILDREN: Corky!

> CORKY: WHAT?

> CHILDREN: COR-KEE!

> CORKY: WELL AWRIGHT!

When it comes to snakes, Corky has a sixth sense. Just as one slithers off the table, he turns and hooks it. The children scream. Corky takes a balloon from Valjean.

> CORKY: Okay, y'all, pay attention. I'm gonna make them snakes strike at me by agitatin' 'em with this here balloon. It's not teasin'; it's just agitatin'. And why am I doing this?

Several hands shoot up enthusiastically. Corky points to one of the boys.

> CORKY: Yes, sir?

> FIRST BOY: You're teachin' us how dangerous the rattler is.

CORKY: Right! That's what I like to hear. And you, sir?

SECOND BOY: You're showin' us how mean they are.

Rose looks skeptical.

CORKY: Gooood. And what does Corky like you to do when he's workin' the rattler?

The children start rhythmically hitting the bleachers with their miniature bats and chanting.

CHILDREN: COR-KEE. COR-KEE. COR-KEE.

The clown skips around the ring with a larger-than-life foam rubber hatchet and pretends to chop the snakes' heads off.

CORKY: And if Corky gets bit, what does he want you to do?

FIRST BOY: Chop the snake's head off!

SECOND BOY: Twist off the rattles and put 'em in your pocket.

The children continue their chant. Corky approaches the table like a cat stalking his prey. He pokes at one of the rattlers with a balloon. The snake coils. The other two snakes try to escape, but Valjean corrals them into the center of the table with his hook.

Corky circles the table. The rattler's head follows his movements. Valjean hands Corky another balloon. Corky pokes at the rattler with the second balloon and the snake strikes, missing both balloons. The children laugh and clap.

The snake coils to strike again. Corky holds one of the balloons a few inches from its face. He jiggles the balloon and the snake makes a direct hit - BOOM! The children scream and jump up and down with excitement.

> CORKY: Awright! Y'all know, twenty years ago, I was afraid of these animals. They affected my job, affected my thinking, affected my sleep. But the Roundup, it made me respect the animal instead of fear it.

Corky tips the table and the snakes slide off. Valjean returns them to their box.

A Junior Snake Wrangler with a snare drum enters the ring and ceremoniously begins to play a drum roll.

Valjean pulls SLINKY, Corky's huge "pet" rattler, out of a box emblazoned with his name spelled out in rhinestones.

> CORKY: Now when somebody says, "Corky, I saw one of your pets today, and I chopped his head off," I say, "gooood." See?

Valjean walks to the table with Slinky dangling from his hook. Suddenly, Slinky undulates violently, alarming the children. Valjean drops him onto the table.

Corky crouches down to snake-eye level and slowly approaches the table. Rose gasps and puts her hand to her mouth.

> CORKY: I used to think that the rattler could do things to me that I know now he can't.

Corky places the end of the balloon in his mouth. Faster drum roll. Slinky coils. They are eye-to-eye. Corky holds absolutely still and Slinky strikes, breaking the balloon. Everyone screams. (A beat) Corky stays crouched and motionless, then turns to the crowd and spits out the balloon. Thunderous applause. Corky eats it up.

>CORKY: Thank y'all. Thank y'all. No snake is ever gonna outsmart Corky.

Corky inches back to the table, leans on it, looks over at Valjean and gives him a little nod. Valjean teases Slinky covertly with his snake hook. Corky's within striking distance. Some of the children notice.

>CHILDREN: Look out, Corky, look out! Stop! STOP!!

As Slinky coils into a tight "S" shape, Corky pretends not to notice what's going on.

>CORKY: Don't worry, Valjean's puttin' ole Slinky back into his box.

CHILDREN: COR-KEE!!!

Too late. Slinky sinks his fangs deep into Corky's forearm. Corky collapses in pain. The children panic. Screaming, they run for the exit. Valjean struggles to release Slinky from his father's arm.

With the help of the clown, Rose tries to corral her stampeding class.

As Rose exits the coliseum, she runs into TOBY, a burly Junior Snake Wrangler, the coliseum's de facto bouncer.

> TOBY: Lemme guess. Corky got bit.
>
> ROSE: Yes! He needs help immediately!
>
> TOBY (to the EMTs): Boys, you're on.

INT. HOSPITAL EMERGENCY ROOM - DAY
Corky lies on a bed. Valjean watches DR. ENNIS roll up Corky's sleeve to reveal a thick, mesh reinforced bandage wrapped around Corky's forearm.

> DR. ENNIS: I swear, Corky Dodds, someday you're gonna forget your snake sleeve and he'll bite you for real.
>
> CORKY: Naw, I wouldn't do nothin' like that.
>
> DR. ENNIS: And you'd best never make Valjean mad—he might forget to milk Slinky first.

Rose appears at the door. Corky rolls down his sleeve and gives Dr. Ennis a "don't blow my cover" look.

> VALJEAN: Why, Miss Rose!
>
> CORKY: It was mighty kind of you to help git me to the hospital so quick, what with all them kids a-screamin' and a-cryin'. Most women would be in hysterics right along side of 'em. Why, a little ole grass snake run my wife plumb out of Eden County.

ROSE: Thank you, Mr. Dodds, but I was pretty concerned about my fourth graders, too. Such histrionics!

CORKY: Well now, that's a mighty big schoolteacher word, but this ain't got nothin' to do with history. I'll set 'em straight, don't you worry.

ROSE: That's why I've come. Why don't you rest for a while. I've scheduled something else for this afternoon.

With a pained look on his face, Corky sits up.

CORKY: Miss Rose, I ain't missed a single Roundup orientatin' class in over twenty years. And this is your first time, ain't it?

ROSE: I've seen snakes before, if that's what you mean. At the Dallas Zoo's herpetarium.

CORKY: Well I ain't talkin' 'bout no tame boa constrictors. What we got here is a hostile, filthy, deadly menace to society.

ROSE: Really, Mr. Dodds? I'd rather you kept that opinion out of my classroom.

CORKY: You're new here, ain't ya? You haven't had the opportunity to experience the rattler yet. So you don't know what I'm talkin' about.

ROSE: If you think you're going to convince me that they hypnotize their prey or chase pregnant women, it's not going to work.

CORKY: Naw, they don't do nothin' like that. Why don't you let me and Valjean here show you?

Embarrassed, Valjean lowers his eyes.

ROSE: I'm not sure you even have snakes here. I haven't seen a single one before today.

CORKY: That's 'cause they've been hibernatin'. You know the big ole oak tree in the town square?

ROSE: Yes?

CORKY: It's got its wake-up call and is startin' to leaf out. It also means the rattler's startin' to stir around in his den. And we like to go in after him before he gits too woke up. We like to seek him out first.

ROSE: Before he seeks you out? Shouldn't the Junior Snake Wranglers be home defending their pregnant wives?

CORKY: Here I am, I just got bit within an inch of my life, and the new schoolteacher's makin' fun of me. We're just tryin' to protect our families, protect our livestock, and our God-given right to this land. We're deliverin' ourselves from evil.

ROSE: Snakes are not evil, Mr. Dodds.

CORKY: Yes, mam, they are. And I'm suggestin' you go on a snake hunt with me so I can prove it to you.

INT. ROSE'S CLASSROOM - DAY

MISS PRITCHETT, a substitute teacher, sits at Rose's desk reading a magazine, ignoring the complete chaos around her. Rose whisks into the room and restores order. SARAH JANE, BOBBY, and PEDRO are students in her class.

> ROSE: Thank you, Miss Pritchett. Everyone in your seats, please.

Miss Pritchett leaves the room.

> SARAH JANE: Is Mr. Corky all right?

> ROSE: He's fine.

> BOBBY: Is he still coming?

> ROSE: I'm afraid not. He'll have to come another day.

The fourth graders are supremely disappointed.

> ROSE: So, we're going to stick to our original lesson plan and review a few facts about snakes. Bobby, what do rattlesnakes eat?

> BOBBY: They eat rats and mice, mam.

> ROSE: That's correct. And what happens if there are not enough snakes to eat the rats and mice? Sarah Jane?

> PEDRO (interrupting): You git lots of 'em in your barn.

ROSE: And why is that bad?

A few hands tentatively are raised. Corky arrives and eavesdrops at the door.

SARAH JANE: Rats can get in your attic, too.

ROSE: Right. So, is it bad to have snakes around?

Corky makes a grand entrance. The children cheer.

CORKY: You bet it is.

ROSE: You've made a quick recovery, Mr. Dodds. We're discussing why it's important to maintain the balance of nature.

CORKY: Miss Rose, if you got rats in your attic, what do you do?

Corky walks around the room, making sure he has everyone's attention.

CORKY: You don't go down to the nearest snake hole and pull yourself out a big, hungry granddaddy of a rattler, take him home, and throw him up in the attic, do you? You buy yourself some rat poison. The rat eats it, gets powerful thirsty, crawls off lookin' for water, and dies in a ditch somewheres. Now, if you had a snake in your attic, he'd eat up all them rats for sure. But you wouldn't want to crawl up there yourself and pull him out. You'd have to find him a big, juicy rat 'bout twice a week to keep him satisfied, then you'd have yourself a pet rattlesnake to take care of for the rest of his life. And snakes can live a long time, Miss Rose.

ROSE: Thank you, Mr. Dodds, but we're talking about cause and effect, not pet rattlesnakes.

CORKY: You started it.

Corky winks at Rose, irritating her even more.

CORKY: Awright class, y'all know I got bit by the rattler today. And y'all was scared that ole Corky wouldn't make it. But here I am standing right in front of you in Miss Rose's classroom. I ain't no ghost.

Corky rubs his arm and looks pained.

CORKY: Now when I got bit, I didn't rub no salted meat into the wound, and I didn't drink no potion of boiled rattlesnake head. We don't believe in them old wives' tales, do we? So who can tell Corky what to do if you get bit by the rattler?

A dozen hands shoot up.

CORKY: That's what I like to see. Yes, sir.

BOBBY: Stay calm.

CORKY: Gooood. And you, sir?

PEDRO: Don't use a tourniquet.

CORKY: Awright! What else?

ROSE (to Corky): The girls have their hands up, too. Sarah Jane?

SARAH JANE: Suck the poison out?

CORKY: Yep.

Corky turns his back to the class, bends over, and points to his rear end.

CORKY: And if you git bit here, that's how you find out who your friends are.

The boys laugh and chant COR-KEE, COR-KEE. The girls lower their eyes in embarrassment.

ROSE (to Corky): You owe Sarah Jane and the rest of the girls an apology.

CORKY (to Rose): Aww, it was just a little ole joke.
(to the class): Boys, I know when my welcome is wore out, so see y'all at the Roundup. Bobby, you still helpin' me out with the snake countin' and weighin'?

BOBBY: Yes, sir!

CORKY: Pedro, the butcherin' and cookin' areas, can I count you in?

PEDRO: Yes, sir, Mr. Corky.

CORKY: And why aren't none of you pretty little girls entered in the Miss Snake Charmer contest?

SARAH JANE: We're not old enough. But my daddy says I'm going to win that someday.

CORKY: You're a right pretty little girl. I hope you do. I hope you do.

EXT./INT. CONVENIENCE STORE - LATE AFTERNOON

Rose pulls into the parking lot.

KUNDOO, an East Indian store manager in his mid-forties, rings up a CUSTOMER's purchases. Kundoo's pet monkey BALI sits contentedly on a perch behind the counter. He wears a collar with a leash that's attached to the perch. Rose enters the store.

KUNDOO: Greetings, Miss Rose.

ROSE: Good afternoon, Kundoo. You were smart to keep Lakshmi home today.

KUNDOO: I heard. The Roundup is not exactly G-rated, so thank you for excusing her from your class. Can I help you find something today?

ROSE: No, thanks, just looking around.

Rose walks aimlessly down an aisle. Her eyes scan the shelves. She finds what she's looking for: the snake bite kits. She lingers, then continues on to a basket of bananas.

After selecting a banana, she returns to the snake bite kits. A **HARRIED CUSTOMER** grabs one off the shelf and pays for it without waiting for the change. Rose tentatively picks one up.

She places her purchases on the counter and Kundoo bags them.

> KUNDOO: Going snake hunting like everyone else?
>
> ROSE: I'm considering it. Just to see what it's all about.
>
> KUNDOO: It will be a good learning experience for the teacher.

Bali stealthily climbs down from his perch and onto the counter. He quietly and methodically opens the paper bag holding Rose's banana.

> KUNDOO: In India, we have deities that are cobras. They roam around wherever they please. Some people even keep them as pets. They feed them milk and little pieces of meat and the cobras are content.

Kundoo notices that Bali has peeled Rose's banana and is eating it.

> KUNDOO: Bali, no! I'm so sorry, Miss Rose. Please go select another banana and take a second one with my compliments.

He scolds Bali, makes him sit on the perch, and shortens his leash.

Rose walks to the far end of the store and chooses two bananas.

Another customer buys a snake kit.

Rose returns to the counter.

> KUNDOO: My curious little monkey is turning the place into an inconvenience store. She loves to unwrap packages.

> ROSE: No harm done, Kundoo. I see why you keep the bananas as far from Bali as possible. This is for him.

Rose hands Bali the second banana.

EXT. EDEN'S LAIR'S MAIN STREET - EARLY EVENING
Rose drives down Main Street. She approaches Eden's Lair's lone, old oak tree—the centerpiece of the town square. Incredulous, she pulls over.

EXT. THE OAK TREE - EARLY EVENING
An enterprising Junior Snake Wrangler's WIFE sells colorful ribbons from a card table. Eden's Lair's MOTHERS and their CHILDREN approach the tree from all directions. They stop a few feet away and solemnly look up into its canopy.

Some of the mothers remove objects from their purses: a baby tooth encased in a sandwich bag; school photographs laminated in plastic; a button from a man's work shirt; an old mum from a daughter's high school prom. A boy tentatively hands his toy pickup truck to his mother. The mothers tie the objects onto the tree with ribbon.

A mother kneels down next to her baby's stroller. The baby's hair is collected into a little ponytail on top of her head. The mother takes out a pair of scissors, snips off the ponytail, and ties it to the tree.

Rose is fascinated by this ritual. The tree is completely decorated with talismans and votive offerings.

EXT. HIGHWAY - NIGHT
Driving down the highway, Rose sees what seems to be Eden's Lair's entire population of pickup trucks parked outside the coliseum.

EXT. COLISEUM - NIGHT
She pulls into the parking lot. Valjean spots her as he gets out of his pickup. He hurries to her car to prevent her from getting out.

>VALJEAN: Miss Rose, what are you doin' here?
>
>ROSE: I was driving home when I saw the lights on in the coliseum, so I thought I'd stop.
>
>VALJEAN: The Roundup don't start 'till tomorrow. They ain't got no snakes in there yet.
>
>ROSE: Then why is every truck in the county parked here?
>
>VALJEAN (looking sheepish): Please, just wait 'till tomorrow. They'll be lots to see then.

Someone opens a door to the coliseum, allowing a swell of men's voices, loud music, and a woman's shriek to escape. Rose opens the car door and takes off in a fast walk toward the coliseum, with Valjean in pursuit.

>VALJEAN: If you want to see some snakes, Corky's got some at the house. I'd be glad to show 'em to you . . . Miss Rose!

INT. COLISEUM - NIGHT
Too late. She's already inside. The coliseum is shoulder-to-shoulder men engaged in serious drinking, gambling, and debauchery.

She sees a woman DANCER gyrating on a 55-gallon drum, wearing chaps and nothing else.

CHUCK, Corky's right-hand man, a tall, burly Junior Snake Wrangler in his mid-thirties, takes flash photos of the woman in chaps.

Rose's face locks into a terrified expression.

A group of DRUNKEN JUNIOR SNAKE WRANGLERS notice Rose and start coming on to her.

> DRUNK JSW: Howdy there, purdy lady. Wanna dance?

The JSW grabs her arm. She stiffens and gasps. Valjean catches up to her.

> VALJEAN: Let go 'a her. C'mon, Miss Rose.

Out of nowhere, Corky, a one-man squall, blasts into the center of the group and into Valjean's face.

> CORKY: Valjean, what the hell are you doing? Git her outta here!

> VALJEAN: Corky, I didn't . . .

CORKY: Do what I say, boy, and do it now. She could have got herself line-balled. You know any woman that shows up the night before the Roundup is fair game. Them's the rules!

Valjean hustles Rose out into the black night.

ROSE: Line-balled?

Valjean puts his blue jean jacket over her shoulders.

VALJEAN: Take is easy, Miss Rose, it's 70 degrees out here and you're shakin' like a baby bird in a blue norther.

Rose removes the jacket and hands it back to Valjean.

ROSE: I'm fine, Valjean, but what about that woman?

Corky catches up with them.

CORKY: Her? She loves to show off, don't she, Valjean? Look, don't get the wrong idea about our little party. It helps the boys get fired up about the Roundup, that's all. It's about all we got to do around here. We're not some big ole fancy place like where you come from. (to Valjean) Make sure she gets home safe. And don't let me see your face again 'till morning.

Bobby and Pedro, Rose's students, come running from the coliseum, giggling. Rose glares at Corky.

EXT. HIGHWAY - NIGHT
Valjean's pickup follows Rose's car. They pass another billboard with a map of Texas and an arrow pointing to Eden's Lair. The

billboard says, "Eden's Lair, Rattlesnake Capital of the World!"

EXT. ROSE'S HOUSE - NIGHT
Rose and Valjean pull up in front of the house. Valjean jumps out of his truck to open Rose's car door.

    VALJEAN: Here we are, safe and sound.

He offers his hand and, hesitating, she takes it.

    ROSE: Thank you, Valjean.

Rose is still shaken from what she saw in the coliseum. They lock eyes for an instant.

    ROSE: Would you like to come in for a cup of coffee?

    VALJEAN: I'd better not, I . . .

    ROSE: Are you sure? You're banished from the coliseum, remember?

    VALJEAN: Coffee sounds good right about now.

As they walk toward the front door, vicious BARKING can be heard coming from inside the house.

    VALJEAN: Dadgum! You protectin' Fort Knox in there?

    ROSE: That's just Bluster. Give me a minute. I'll take him upstairs and put the water on for coffee.

Rose enters the house. BLUSTER slips past her and slams his body against the screen door. Valjean jumps back. Rose closes the wooden front door.

INT. ROSE'S BEDROOM/BATHROOM - NIGHT
Rose drags Bluster into the room by his collar and flips on the light. In her absence, Bluster has destroyed the room.

    ROSE: Bad dog!

She reaches down and picks up her students' homework—torn to shreds. She bursts into tears.

Looking in the bathroom mirror, Rose blots her eyes with a tissue.

    ROSE: (whispers) Pull yourself together. You've got a guest downstairs.

EXT. ROSE'S HOUSE - NIGHT
She opens the front door, holding a fist-full of chewed-up papers.

Valjean is checking the hinges on the door of her tornado shelter.

    ROSE: Just look at this! Now "the dog ate my homework" excuse doesn't seem so flimsy.

    VALJEAN: It always worked for me.

He smiles radiantly and winks at Rose.

    ROSE: Come on in.

INT. ROSE'S KITCHEN - NIGHT
Valjean eagerly follows Rose into the kitchen.

>ROSE: Make yourself at home.

>VALJEAN: Thank you, mam.

He pulls out a kitchen chair and sits down. Rose pours the coffee. Two white doves COO softly in a cage.

>VALJEAN: They make a mighty purdy pair.

>ROSE: I've had them for a long time. I couldn't bear to leave them back in Dallas.

>VALJEAN: I bet you left lots of important things behind.

>ROSE: Nothing I couldn't live without. Like my high heels and my fancy car. (A beat) What if we could move to a new place and not have to drag the past along with us?

Rose has initiated a conversation she didn't intend to and nervously stirs her coffee.

>VALJEAN: I think about that a lot, too. But what made you want to move out *here*? Seems like a woman like you'd have better places to go.

>ROSE: Well who wouldn't want to live in Eden? No sin, no shame, no crime, no violence.

Lightning illuminates the kitchen, followed by a loud CLAP of thunder. Rose jumps. Reflexively, Valjean leaps from his chair and places a protective hand on her shoulder. He detours to look out the window.

> VALJEAN: This ain't that kind of Eden, that's for sure. It's a hell of a place.

She joins him at the window.

> ROSE: You don't seem 100% on-board with the Roundup.

> VALJEAN: I tried to escape by joining the Army, but Eden's Lair's got me on a short leash. I'd like to be more than Corky Dodds's son someday.

Another crash of thunder. The sky bursts open.

> VALJEAN: I'd better get going or I'll have to sleep on the couch. Bluster wouldn't like that.

> ROSE: But I would.

She didn't intend to let that slip. They look longingly at each other, and she gives him a quick, awkward hug, her head lingering on his chest for a beat. She pulls away.

> VALJEAN: Let me move them birds away from the window in case we get pounded with some of that baseball-sized hail. It's that time of year.

Valjean moves the cage away from the window.

> ROSE: Another Eden's Lair claim to fame?

VALJEAN: Oh, yes, mam. Killer tornadoes, too. If it sounds like a train's coming, get yourself down into the tornado shelter, pronto. Can we do this again sometime?

ROSE: Yes. I'd like that.

She extends her hand to shake his, and he pulls her toward him. But when he notices a slight hesitation, he reins in his passion and lets go. He pivots and heads for the front door, then turns to look at Rose one last time.

VALJEAN: Are you okay?

She nods tentatively. He's almost out the door.

ROSE: Valjean?

VALJEAN: Miss Rose?

ROSE: Does "line-balled" mean what I think it means?

VALJEAN: Naw, forget it. That's just Roundup talk.

Rose doesn't buy it.

VALJEAN: I'll come by tomorrow and tighten the hinges on your tornado shelter. Make sure they're good and secure.

Another crash of thunder. Valjean disappears into the night.

INT. ROSE'S BEDROOM - NIGHT
Bluster curls up against the bedroom door while Rose, dressed for bed in a long-sleeved nightgown, locks the door. A hard rain falls on her home's corrugated tin roof, making a deafening sound.

She walks to the window. Distant lightning illuminates enormous thunderheads and the prairie. The drone of the rain and the flashes of lightning mesmerize Rose.

INTERCUT - EXT. DALLAS STREET - NIGHT
Rain pounds Rose as she walks down a street lined with nightclubs and restaurants. Bursts of sound and music emerge as she passes each club. The heels of her shoes make a frightened, rhythmic TAPPING. She searches her pockets for her keys, unsuccessfully. She arrives at her car, pitches her purse on the hood. Digs frantically through the purse. POV a hand on her shoulder.

BACK TO SCENE
Her cell phone rings. A trembling hand picks it up from the night stand.

>   ROSE: Hello?

INTERCUT - INT.
Corky calls from a pay phone in a bar.

>   CORKY: Miss Rose? This here's Corky. Just wanted to make sure you got home okay.

>   ROSE: Yes, I'm home, thanks.

>   CORKY: I also wanted to apologize for the little misunderstanding earlier.

>   ROSE: I'm pretty sure I understood what was going on.

CORKY: Them boys was just blowin' off a little steam, that's all. It didn't upset you, did it?

ROSE: It's not fourth grade field trip material, that's for sure.

CORKY: It's mighty good to hear you got your sense of humor back. Look, the boys get together once a year and things get a little rowdy. The other 364 days they're at home with their wives and children being good husbands and fathers. It's not too much to begrudge a fella, is it? They didn't mean no harm. Let's drop it, whadda you say?

Chuck is in the b.g. stifling laughter.

ROSE: I appreciate the apology, but . . .

CORKY: Look, you're gonna hunt the rattler with me, ain't you?

ROSE: I haven't said I would. I'm still thinking about it.

CORKY: Well, tomorrow I got more work than you can shake a snake hook at. How about after church on Sunday?

ROSE: I'll give you an answer tomorrow. Good night, Mr. Dodds.

Rose hangs up. With a frozen expression, she stares into the distance.

EXT. EDEN'S LAIR'S MAIN STREET - LATE MORNING
The very inept Eden's Lair High School marching band leads a meager parade. The 4-H Club's winning steers follow the band.

A young future rancher leads a huge Brahman bull by the nose ring while his assistant gently strokes the bull's testicles, to keep him pacified, with one of the miniature baseball bats that were passed out at the coliseum.

Following is a float that transports last year's "Miss Snake Charmer," JEW-ELLE, who wears red spike heels, a red swimsuit, a purple robe with a snakeskin collar, and a crown. She smiles and waves mechanically at the crowd.

In her wake are the contestants vying for this year's title, wearing yellow swimsuits. Traversing their torsos are red streamers that advertise their sponsors: "The Social Butterfly," "Tacos de Tomas," "Patti Parties," "Lu-Ann's Dance Studio and Gift Shop," "Eden's Lair Auto Parts."

Rose watches the parade. Sarah Jane, the fourth grader humiliated by Corky, sees Rose and drags her mom PATTI SCROGIE through the crowd to introduce the two women.

> SARAH JANE: Miss Rose, Miss Rose! This here's my mom; I want you to meet her.

They shake hands.

> PATTI: It's a pleasure, Miss Rose.

> ROSE: Nice to meet you, Mrs. Scrogie. Sarah Jane is one of my best students.

> PATTI: She told me how purdy you were! Ever bit of it's true.

SARAH JANE: There's sister. Look, look!

ROSE: Which one is she?

SARAH JANE: Right there! Patti Parties. (chanting and clapping her hands) Patti Parties, Patti Parties.

PATTI: It's my little business I do while the girls are at school. At first my husband didn't want me to work, but then he decided he liked the extra beer money.

ROSE: What kind of parties do you organize?

PATTI: Mainly pony parties for the kids, quinceañeros—I can't never say that word right!—for the fifteen-year-old Mexican girls. This time of year is the busiest, what with the Roundup and ever-thang, and I even help with that.

Rose registers shock: did Patti have something to do with last night's party in the coliseum?

SARAH JANE: Mom, Mr. Corky said I should be in the Miss Snake Charmer contest. Just like sister.

PATTI: You gotta be at least eighteen years old. Them's the rules. You still got a few years to go, girl.

In the parade of contestants, Rose notices a girl reminiscent of Valjean: DARLYNN DOBBS. She looks pale and a little distant, but, clearly, she is the most beautiful contestant of the group.

ROSE: Who's the girl wearing the "Dodds U-Haul" banner?

PATTI: Oh, that's Darlynn. Corky's daughter.

ROSE: Corky has a daughter? I had no idea.

PATTI: Nobody talks about Darlynn much. We just let her go on about her business.

ROSE: She's very beautiful.

PATTI: Yeah, I reckon so. But she's kinda funny in the head. Keeps to herself mostly. Miss Rose, we're having a little cookout later on. Would you care to join us?

SARAH JANE: Oh, please? Please come. It's my birthday.

ROSE: Thank you very much, Mrs. Scrogie, I'd love to.

Valjean pushes his way through the crowd to Rose.

VALJEAN: Miss Rose, I've been looking all over for you.

ROSE: I've been right here rooting for your sister.

VALJEAN: Darlynn? She don't need none of that. She knows she ain't gonna win; she's Corky's daughter and that'd be favoritism. Besides, when they start askin' her all them questions, she's gonna freeze up. Don't get me wrong, Miss Rose, I love my sister, I just know her, that's all.

A cloud comes over Valjean's face.

VALJEAN: There's more important things goin' on at the moment. Corky texted that I should come fetch you, pronto.

ROSE: If this is about hunting snakes, I told him I haven't made up my mind.

VALJEAN: Corky says its urgent.

ROSE (skeptical): All right. Excuse us, please, Mrs. Scrogie. Bye, Sarah Jane.

SARAH JANE: See you later, Miss Rose.

Valjean and Rose work their way through the crowd.

VALJEAN: Corky says you don't believe in the danger of the rattler.

ROSE: Not in the way he talks about them. Not in the Biblical sense.

VALJEAN: Some of them stories is a bit far-fetched. But there ain't nothin' Biblical about this.

ROSE: So where are we going?

VALJEAN: Down below the 'scarpment. You don't even have to get out of the pickup. Don't worry; I'll never make you do nothing you don't want to do. And I'll see to it that Corky don't neither.

ROSE: I made a commitment to Sarah Jane. Promise I'll be back in time?

VALJEAN: Come hell or high water.

INT. VALJEAN'S PICKUP - MIDDAY
Rose looks out the window at the town scenery. They pass a fast food restaurant sign that says, "Sink Your Fangs Into Our Delicious Fried Chicken," and a Dairy Queen sign that says, "For a Tasty Treat That Won't Bite Back, Stop Here!"

Dodd's U-Haul, Corky's business, comes into view. A sign above the entrance to the building says "Snake Hooks, Burlap Bags, Gas Canisters, Pocket Mirrors. I got it all!" The parking lot is choked with rattlesnake hunters renting small U-Hauls.

Chuck and his sidekick STEVE, another Junior Snake Wrangler in his late twenties with long, greasy blond hair, hand out snake hunting supplies to a group of hunters. As Rose and Valjean pass by in the truck, Chuck and Steve glare at Valjean and turn their backs.

ROSE: The family business, I take it? Who runs the store during Roundup weekend?

VALJEAN: Chuck and Steve mostly. My mom used to, 'fore she left Eden's Lair. I was real proud of her. She was the only woman I ever knew who would skin a rattlesnake. Course they stopped her from doin' it.

ROSE: Who did?

VALJEAN: The Junior Snake Wranglers. None of 'em would touch a dead rattlesnake 'till they seen her do it. Then they said, "if a woman can do it, so can we." So Corky let 'em take it over. After that, she did all the cookin'.

ROSE: Is that what this "urgent" thing is about? The Roundup is short of cooks?

VALJEAN: A woman can skin snakes all day long as far as I'm concerned. But a man cook? Now that takes a talent not too many of us has.

Valjean turns onto a dusty road. Out of view of Rose, his phone lights up with a text message from Corky: "Stall. Ten more minutes." Valjean is delighted: more alone time with Rose.

VALJEAN: Mind if we stop here for a minute? I want to show you something.

ROSE: Okay. Sure.

He pulls up to the edge of the escarpment that overlooks Eden's Lair and takes the opportunity to open up to Rose.

VALJEAN: It's not much like the real Eden's supposed to be, but I love this view. It reminds me of the Hollywood you see in the movies. It's night; convertibles are parked all along the cliff and everybody's lookin' at the twinkling lights and watchin' them spotlights criss-crossin' in the sky. It makes you start wonderin' about life. How you fit in.

Valjean's phone lights up again but he misses it.

VALJEAN: 'Cause when you drive back down the hill you become part of the excitement, but you don't quite see it that-a-way. When you're in it, lookin' at it up-close, it's just everyday life. The noise, the people, the bull you gotta put up with. Takes away the magic. That's why the Roundup means so much to folks around here. It's like being up on top of the Hollywood cliff. Takin' a vacation from life for a while.

Off in the distance, Corky CALLS for Valjean.

VALJEAN: Gol durn it, it's Corky.

The pickup bounces down the hill to the plain below.

EXT. CREEK BED - AFTERNOON
Corky stands beside a huge Hereford steer lying on the ground panting. Dr. Ennis ministers to it.

Valjean and Rose exit the pickup. Corky angrily storms up to Valjean.

CORKY: Valjean Dodds, didn't I tell you to bring Miss Rose here ASAP? What were you doing dilly-dallying up there on the cliff?

VALJEAN: I'm sorry, sir; I was just . . .

ROSE: Hello Dr. Ennis. I didn't expect to see you here.

DR. ENNIS: Corky asked me to make a house call. This steer is in pretty bad shape.

ROSE: What's wrong with him?

CORKY: Miss Rose, over here, please. Walk slow so he don't get no more upset than he already is. Easy, easy.

Rose approaches the steer cautiously.

CORKY: Looky here.

Corky points out two small, bleeding puncture wounds in the steer's neck. Rose gasps.

ROSE: What happened?

CORKY: Well it weren't Dracula. Smell that musty odor? It's the rattler. Just missed the jugular.

ROSE: Will he be okay?

CORKY: We'll just have to wait and see. Ole doc here can't very well put a tourniquet around his neck, now can he?

ROSE: How did it happen?

CORKY: As far as I know, rattlers can't jump. Thank goodness the good Lord didn't give 'em no legs.

ROSE: He was grazing.

CORKY: I swear, Miss Rose, you ain't no schoolteacher for nothin'. That's how most of 'em git bit out here. They're too stupid to know a coiled rattler from a cow pie.

The steer groans and thrashes. Corky and Dr. Ennis struggle to keep him under control.

> CORKY: Valjean, throw me your rifle. We'd better put him out of his misery.

Valjean walks back to his truck and pulls an M16 rifle out from behind the seat.

> ROSE: Wait! There's nothing else you can do?

Valjean hands the M16 over to Corky.

> CORKY: No, mam.

> ROSE: Valjean, take me back to town, please.

> VALJEAN: Yes, mam.

Rose angrily marches toward the pickup. Corky plants a foot on the steer's body.

> CORKY: Miss Rose! I'm just trying to make a point!

She climbs into the pickup and slams the door.

> CORKY: I know how much you teachers like them learnin' experiences. I thought you'd appreciate this!

> ROSE: I already know enough about suffering.

> CORKY: Are you still going to hunt the rattler with me?

Valjean turns on the ignition, and the pickup disappears in a wake of dust.

>   DR. ENNIS: Get off that steer, Corky, before he wakes up and throws you off.

Corky and Dr. Ennis give each other sly looks, then burst out laughing. Corky cocks the rifle and points it straight up in the air.

CUT TO INT. VALJEAN'S PICKUP
Rose flinches as she hears the sound of the gun discharge.

EXT. SCROGIE BACK YARD - AFTERNOON
A banner on the back porch says, "Patti Parties Presents Sarah Jane's 9th Birthday!" Sarah Jane's CLASSMATES eat, drink lemonade, and laugh. The FATHERS sit in lawn chairs and drink beer. Sarah Jane's father EARL SCROGIE grills hot dogs and hamburgers, and the WIVES dutifully deliver the food to their husbands.

Rose comes through the chain-link gate with a present under her arm. Patti Scrogie eagerly approaches her.

>   PATTI: Miss Rose, I'm so glad you could make it. Would you like a hot dog? How 'bout a hamburger?

The thought of eating a hamburger makes Rose vaguely nauseated.

>   ROSE: No, thank you. But something to drink sounds good.

>   PATTI: EARL!

Earl Scrogie looks supremely put-out as he puts his barbecue tools down and opens the ice chest.

> PATTI (to Rose): What'd you think of our girl? We're so proud of her, we could just bust.
>
> ROSE: You have many reasons to be proud of Sarah Jane. She's very bright.
>
> PATTI: Oh, I mean Suzie, her sister. She's gonna be our next Miss Snake Charmer.

Patti lets out a little squeal of delight. Earl arrives with a couple of beers. He opens one with his teeth and hands it to Rose.

> EARL: Afternoon, Miss Rose. You're lookin' mighty purdy today yourself.
>
> PATTI: Do you always have to do that little trick of yours, Earl?
>
> EARL: Patti here ruins all my fun.
>
> PATTI: I'm sure Miss Rose don't want your spittle in her beer.
>
> ROSE: Actually, I was on my way over to the lemonade. Excuse me.

Rose heads for the refreshment table. The men look her up and down. Earl grabs Patti by the arm.

> EARL: Don't you never say nothin' like that again in front of my daughter's schoolteacher. Ever. You hear me?

Sarah Jane sees Rose pouring herself some lemonade and skips up to the table.

> SARAH JANE: Miss Rose!
>
> ROSE: Happy birthday, Sarah Jane.

She hands Sarah Jane her present. She opens it: a copy of the book *Strong is the New Pretty*. Sarah Jane tries to hide her disappointment.

> SARAH JANE: Oh. I don't get it, but thanks a lot anyway.

Sarah Jane skips over to a card table where all her presents sit. She places the book among the Barbie doll clothes, make-up kits, play jewelry, and a pair of little girl's glittery high heel shoes.

The mothers file into Patti Scrogie's living room through a sliding glass door. Sarah Jane skips back over to Rose.

> SARAH JANE: The girls are gonna do a practice session for tonight. Come on!

Rose follows Sarah Jane into the living room.

INT. LIVING ROOM - AFTERNOON

The mothers seat themselves in folding chairs placed around the perimeter of the room. A white sheet serves as a curtain between the living room and the kitchen. Painted on the sheet with glitter are the words "Miss Snake Charmer: We'll Put a Spell on You." Lots of GIGGLING and shuffling around in the kitchen. Patti motions to Rose to sit beside her.

PATTI: The girls do this every year to help calm their nerves. It don't do much for ours, though.

ROSE: Where's Darlynn? Is she here?

PATTI: Nah. She don't never want to git involved in things. I think it's just plain snootiness. Just 'cause she's Corky Dodds's daughter, she thinks she's better than everyone else.

ROSE: Why did she enter the contest?

PATTI: Beats me! The girls don't like her, she don't have no personality. Nobody thinks she has a lick of a chance.

INT. PATTI'S KITCHEN - AFTERNOON
The Miss Snake Charmer contestants have transformed the kitchen into an elaborate dressing room. EDNA, one of the mothers, advises the girls on their makeup. Her own features are almost unrecognizable for the amount of makeup she has applied to them.

EDNA: Now tonight, you'll look white under those bright lights. So, darken your makeup; use darker lipstick. Just double everything to extremes.

Edna reaches for a large, fluffy brush and a cake of blush.

EDNA: Vicki, you need more blush. You, too, Vanessa. And don't forget that jar of Vaseline. Someone ought to put it where you can grab some on your way out to the stage.

INT. LIVING ROOM - AFTERNOON
ANGEL, a six-year-old Mexican boy, is forced out from behind the curtain. He wears a little tuxedo and top hat and carries a

cheap wireless microphone. The mothers giggle. Sarah Jane dims the room lights, stands on a chair, and trains a bright flashlight onto Angel.

> ANGEL: Ladies and gentlemen. Tonight, we present the most beautiful girls in the entire world. The contestants for this year's Miss Snake Charmer of the Eden's Lair's Rattlesnake Roundup.

"Man! I Feel Like a Woman" (Shania Twain) plays on a boom box. Angel reads the list of names as best he can, while each girl emerges from behind the curtain wearing her evening gown. The mothers applaud enthusiastically. Patti turns to Rose with tears in her eyes.

> PATTI: This is one of the best days of my life.

The girls practice their twirls and turns and smiles. One mother motions for her daughter to come to her. The girl bends over and the mother rubs a bit of lipstick off her teeth. The girls line up single-file and parade out into the yard for the men's approval.

EXT. SCROGIE BACK YARD - AFTERNOON
The girls line up chorus-line style. The men let out an Indian war cry. The line breaks and each daughter runs to her father. Some sit on their father's knees, other fathers scoop up their daughters and twirl them around. Fathers and daughters all dance while the mothers remain indoors. Rose watches uncomfortably from the sliding glass door as a drunken father kisses his daughter a little too eagerly on the neck.

INT. COLISEUM - AFTERNOON
A snake pit. Corky stands ankle-deep in rattlesnakes and uses an electrified megaphone to talk to his audience. The sound of the rattlers is like bacon FRYING in a huge skillet.

> CORKY: The rattlesnake are not becoming extinct in any respect. They're more or less holding their own, even gaining on us in population in certain areas. Those are the areas we concentrate on. We're just trying to control the species.

Valjean walks up to the pit carrying a thirty-gallon metal trash can and dumps its contents—a knot of rattlesnakes—into the pit.

The slaughter area. A large, bloody tree stump. Toby, the burly Junior Snake Wrangler bouncer, dressed in a white lab coat splattered with blood, chops snakes' heads off while another JSW, ADAM, talks to a small group.

> ADAM: I used to think they're not good for anything else, so it would tickle me to death to cut their heads off. 'Cause I thought, they're dangerous anyhow and that's what we want to do with them. Now, it's just like cuttin' off a chicken's head. Except that snakes are easier to catch.

A group of curious BOYS watch. Toby throws the snake heads into a bucket. The snakes' mouths open and shut reflexively.

> BOY: Those heads are still moving. Let us have a head! Chop another one's head off!

The skinning area. Several Junior Snake Wranglers are skinning decapitated snakes. JASON, a JSW, talks to a group.

> JASON: They're very easy to skin. The hide just slips right off. You take them insides out and it's just in a plastic bag. And that plastic bag comes right on out and you got them entrails in there all neat and tidy.

A table displays rattlesnake products: snakeskin hat bands and belts, key chains with rattles, rattlesnake head paperweights, and a rattlesnake embedded in the lid of a clear Lucite toilet seat.

A JSW's WIFE sews the mouth of a live rattlesnake shut. Her HUSBAND takes the writhing snake from her and places it around the shoulders of a LITTLE BOY. The little boy's PARENTS already have snakes around their shoulders. They sit in front of a faux Wild West background. They pose. A PHOTOGRAPHER takes their picture, flash —

INT. AUDITORIUM STAGE - NIGHT
To reveal Edna—she has just taken a group photo of the Snake Charmer contestants. They're lined up behind the curtain; it's moments until show time. Vicki slathers Vaseline on her teeth. Edna gives them a last-minute pep talk.

> EDNA: Don't forget to smile. Vicki, you look worried, relax! Hold your stomach in, Maria. And Louann, don't walk like you're headed for the nearest bathroom.

The girls giggle nervously. Edna hushes the girls and jogs off-stage.

The front of the curtain. BOB, the Master of Ceremonies, a toupee-sporting, middle-age local TV personality, walks on stage wearing a (costume) suit of armor and carrying a lance. Corky enters from the opposite side dragging a wooden box. The audience laughs and cheers.

Valjean enters the auditorium from the back and looks around. He spots Rose. She's sitting with Sarah Jane and her mother Patti. Patti clutches a large bouquet of red roses wrapped in cellophane.

Corky and Bob step up to the mic. Because of his limited vision, Bob almost knocks over the mic stand.

> CORKY: What's with the get-up, Bob? You been out fightin' dragons or somethin'?

Bob mumbles something unintelligible. Corky knocks on Bob's helmet. Bob raises the visor.

> CORKY: Bob, take that durn thing off so I can hear you. And so you can see.

Bob shakes his head "no."

> CORKY: Come on now, Bob. Give me the lance, too. I forgot my snake hook back at the truck.

Bob clutches the lance close to his body, steps away from the mic, and starts to shake.

> CORKY: Some dragon fighter you are.

Corky shades his eyes from the bright light and looks out into the audience.

> CORKY: Valjean, you back there, boy? Git me my snake hook.

Several eager young boys' hands shoot up from the audience.

>BOYS: We'll get it, Corky. Let us get it!

>VALJEAN (under his breath): Same ole routine.

>CORKY: Awright, but you boys be careful out there. I mighta forgot and left some big ole granddaddy snake in the front seat.

The girls in the audience scream. The adults laugh.

Cautiously, Bob tiptoes over to the mic stand, grabs it, and quickly retreats to his comfort zone.

>BOB: Welcome everyone to the . . . my heart's pounding so hard I can hardly remember. Which one is it, Corky?

A banner that reads "25th Eden's Lair Rattlesnake Roundup", descends from above. The previous year's Miss Snake Charmer Jew-Elle, dressed in her coronation cloak and crown, comes on stage. The audience cheers.

>BOB: Ladies and gentlemen, last year's Miss Snake Charmer, Jew-Elle Jones; it's still Jones, right?

>JEW-ELLE: Yes, but not for long!

She squeals, and waves to the audience showing off the engagement ring on her left hand. She hands Corky a wireless mic, and Corky gives her a little peck on the cheek.

CORKY: Test, test, thanks, darlin'. It's the 25th, Bob, see? Come on, let's say it all together.

The audience joins in.

CORKY (with the audience): Eden's Lair Rattlesnake Round-up.

BOB: While we're waiting for that snake hook . . .

Bob "knocks" on the curtain.

BOB: You don't mind waiting a little longer, girls, do you?

He turns the mic around to pick up the muffled protestations from behind the curtain.

CORKY: 'Course they don't, Bob. Now let's check in with our very special guest. Take the mic down and see if we can hear him rattlin'.

BOB: You do the honors, Corky.

Corky holds the wireless mic close to the box. Nothing. He nudges the box with his foot. No response. Corky kicks the box. An ominous BUZZING noise arises.

BOB: It's rattling, isn't it?

CORKY: Yes, sir-ee.

BOB: Good. I didn't know if it was him or my knees.

The boys come on stage with Corky's snake hook. Corky opens the box and waves them over. They hesitate. They come only so close, then lay the snake hook down and run off stage.

>CORKY: Thank you, boys.

Corky turns to the audience. One of the snakes slowly starts to emerge from the box.

>CORKY: Now, I want to emphasize that picking up a rattler is a very dangerous business.

AUDIENCE: Corky, turn around!

Bob backs away and runs off stage. He re-enters with a two-by-four.

>CORKY: In the course of my career, I've been nicked and scratched over fifty times . . . you mad at me about somethin', Bob?

Bob points to the snake. Corky springs into action—tosses the mic to Jew-Elle, scoops up the snake, and slams it back into the box. He steps on the tail of another snake that is slithering away and grabs it with his snake hook. The giant, dangling rattlesnake starts to undulate, making graceful S-curves and alarming the audience.

>BOB: No, Corky, you're a charming man. I can't say much for the company you keep, however.

Jew-Elle hands the mic back to Corky.

CORKY: Thank you, Bob. I'll just take my friends off-stage now. They'll be in your dressing room.

The audience shrieks and applauds. Patti Scrogie applauds eagerly, elbowing Rose. Rose smiles politely, then looks down at her hands folded neatly in her lap. Valjean watches her from the back of the auditorium.

Bob lopes off-stage. The banner is raised and the curtain parts. Two spotlights scan the contestants who are doing a very poorly executed high-kick routine and singing:

CONTESTANTS: "Thank heaven for little girls/ Thank heaven for them all, no matter where no matter who/Without them what would little boys do . . . "

All of them sing, except for Darlynn. Her solemn, pale face contrasts with the others' exaggerated make-up and Vaseline-enhanced smiles.

The curtain closes and Bob enters wearing a Liberace-style jacket. He holds a packet of index cards.

BOB: Tonight, twenty-two young ladies, the most beguiling in the entire world, are gracing our stage. Two hours from now, all of you will be gone and among this list of cards, only one name will be left. Hold not your tears for the winner; hold your tears for the twenty-one who will have to be taken out before the night is over.

The curtain opens.

BOB: Contestant number one is Tammy Ball.

TAMMY appears in a shimmering bathing suit and spike heels she can barely walk in.

BOB: Tammy is known as "Baby Doll". She is five feet four, weighs 115, and is sponsored by the K-Bob Steak House. You didn't ply the judges with a big, juicy T-bone last night, did you?

Tammy gets the giggles—in her shoulders.

BOB: Tammy is a senior at Eden's Lair High School, she wants to be a religious counselor or a Kindergarten teacher. She likes to listen to the radio and to crochet and sew. She eats salad, pizza, and steak, loves the LeAnn Rimes "It's Christmas Eve" soundtrack, and is waging a one-girl campaign to get Led Zeppelin banned from the radio.

Her family cheers from the audience.

BOB: Contestant number two is Darlynn Dodds.

A polite but lukewarm reaction from the audience.

BOB: Now, everyone already knows who Darlynn Dodds is.

INTERCUT

PATTI (to Rose): It just ain't right for Darlynn to be in the Miss Snake Charmer contest. It's favoritism, clear as day.

BACK TO SCENE

BOB: And for this special occasion, Corky has written his own portrayal of Darlynn. Corky, come out here and do the honors.

Corky walks on stage and as he reads, Darlynn mechanically walks, spins, and twirls. The heels of her shoes make a loud, tapping noise on the wooden stage.

CORKY: "Darlynn is five foot-six, weighs 120 pounds, and measures out about the same as Marilyn Monroe. Her favorite pastimes include shoppin' for my wardrobe, pickin' up after me, and makin' sure there's a hot meal waitin' when I get home from a hard day's work. In the fall, she'll be attending Eden's Lair Junior College so she can be close to home, and someday, she wants to marry someone just like her Daddy."

The audience laughs at Darlynn's expense.

BOB: Corky, you always were a sentimentalist.

Darlynn doesn't react; she just keeps walking and twirling.

Rose covers her eyes with her hands.

PATTI: Are you all right, Miss Rose?

ROSE: I'm feeling a little dizzy, that's all. Excuse me.

Rose shuffles past the people in her row, looking troubled as she makes her way to the aisle.

INT. AUDITORIUM HALLWAY - NIGHT
Rose's shoes make a sharp, hollow sound in the deserted hallway. Muffled APPLAUSE sounds vaguely like rain falling on pavement.

INTERCUT - EXT. DALLAS STREET - NIGHT
Rain drenches Rose as she walks down a street. The heels of her shoes make an insistent, rhythmic tapping. She arrives at her car; pitches her purse on the hood. Digs frantically through the purse. A hand on her shoulder. It spins her around. Rose's face is pure horror.

BACK TO SCENE
Rose collapses onto the terrazzo floor.

INT. AUDITORIUM STAGE - NIGHT

>   BOB: This is one of the tougher moments of tonight. After they're called up, each of our top finalists will be asked a question.

Bob walks solemnly up to Tammy.

>   BOB: Tammy Ball, which type would you rather be with, Billy Bob Thornton or Russell Crowe, and explain.

>   TAMMY: Well, they're both pretty good. Russell Crowe, he's pretty protective and everything; but Billy Bob, he's a whole lotta fun. He would take you out on the town and show you the best night of your life, like in that movie *Daddy and Them*. I think it'd be a really great time.

BOB: Maria Martinez, what is more important for a girl—good looks or a gracious personality?

MARIA: I think it don't matter how she looks, if she's purdy or if she's not so purdy. It's just the way how she carries herself.

BOB: Okay. Suzie Scrogie.

The audience applauds for Suzie. Corky scrutinizes her from the wings.

BOB: What would be your ideal man?

SUZIE: Everybody's idea man is tall, dark, and handsome, but I guess if you got down to marrying somebody, you'd want someone who is brave and loyal and would just take real good care of you.

The audience roots for Suzie. To be heard above the clapping, Sarah Jane strikes the back of Rose's vacant chair. A tear rolls down Patti's cheek.

BOB: Okay. Darlynn.

Corky stands in the wings looking nervous.

Valjean notices the vacant seat and looks around for Rose. He leaves the auditorium.

BOB: Tell us what your daddy said about you entering the Miss Snake Charmer contest.

A long, uncomfortable pause.

>DARLYNN: He don't want me to win. But I do.

Corky bounds on stage.

>CORKY: Naw, Darlynn, I didn't say no such thing. You know it would make Corky proud as all heck if you won. A pretty girl like you! I was just behavin' like a father worrying about his daughter. Worrying about the initiation. You know if you win, you got to milk the biggest, juiciest, granddaddy of a rattlesnake that we can find. Ain't that right, Jew-Elle?

Looking vaguely frightened, Jew-Elle nods. The audience laughs and applauds. Corky whisks Darlynn off-stage before she can say anything else.

>CORKY: Thank y'all. Thank y'all.

INT. AUDITORIUM HALLWAY - NIGHT
Valjean sees Rose lying unconscious and takes off in a run toward her. He skids to a stop on his knees and gently lifts her head. She regains consciousness.

>VALJEAN: Miss Rose! Are you all right?

>ROSE: I think so. I could use a drink of water.

>VALJEAN: Let me set you on this here bench first, and I'll git you some water.

Valjean picks her up and their eyes lock. Tenderly, he places her on a bench. He cradles her shoulders in his jacket and bursts out of the auditorium.

INT. AUDITORIUM STAGE - NIGHT
Bob and Jew-Elle stand at the microphone.

> BOB: You've had one year of being Queen; you've already told us publicly and privately that you don't want to give it up.

> JEW-ELLE: No, I surely don't.

> BOB: Somehow, the show must go on, right?

> JEW-ELLE: Right.

> BOB: What did they say at Texas Tech when you said, "I gotta take a couple days off to be Rattlesnake Queen."

> JEW-ELLE: Snake Queen, what's THAT?

The audience loves this.

> BOB: Ready to crown our new queen?

Jew-Elle fights tears. She nods bravely.

> BOB: Our old queen will crown her, and our new queen will reign. Contestant number five, Suzie Scrogie.

Screams of delight. The contestants graciously embrace Suzie. Darlynn stands self-consciously apart from the group.

Corky enters from off-stage, wearing a king's crown, a purple robe with gold trim, and holding his snake hook like a scepter.

He waves to the audience. Suzie is positioned in between Bob and Corky. The audience gives her a standing ovation.

The photographer appears on stage. He rubs some lipstick off Suzie's teeth and takes the trio's picture.

INT. AUDITORIUM HALLWAY - NIGHT
Rose drinks water out of a plastic bottle that says "Kundoo's Konvenience Store."

> VALJEAN: Are you feeling better now?

> ROSE: I don't know what happened. All I remember is the sound of your voice.

The auditorium doors fly open and people stream out. Earl and Patti Scrogie and Sarah Jane see Rose and Valjean sitting together on the bench. Sarah Jane skips up to them.

> SARAH JANE: Suzie won! Suzie won! And I'm going to win someday, too.

Patti is so emotional she can barely speak. She holds the bouquet of roses wrapped in cellophane.

> PATTI: We're so proud of our girl. Will you come to the house for the victory party? You, too, Valjean, if you'd like.

> ROSE: I'm afraid I'm not feeling all that well. But please tell Suzie congratulations for me.

> PATTI: We sure will. If you change your mind, we'll be partyin' to the wee hours so come on over.

(To Valjean) Give Darlynn our condolences.

VALJEAN: Yes, mam.

SARAH JANE: Here, Miss Rose. To make you feel better.

Sarah Jane pulls a single rose out of Suzie's bouquet and hands it to Rose. The SOUND of the cellophane wrapper triggers a memory.

INTERCUT - INT. HOSPITAL EXAMINATION ROOM - NIGHT
Wearing a hospital gown, her hand resting in the hand of a NURSE, Rose is helped down from an examination table. She leaves behind a red smear on the thin, CRINKLY paper covering the table.

Through the window, RICHARD, her husband, his head bandaged, is seen pacing back and forth in the hallway. Richard, early thirties, has handsome, intense dark eyes and a rugged physique.

BACK TO SCENE

PATTI: 'Scuse us. We gotta get backstage now and congratulate her ourselves. You take it easy.

Chuck and Steve talk with a group of Junior Snake Wranglers. Corky approaches the group and slips a small vial into Chuck's hand. Chuck looks over at Valjean and Rose and sneers, while Steve combs his long, greasy hair.

Corky approaches Eden's Lair's SHERIFF and inserts a bulky envelope into an inner pocket of his jacket.

>VALJEAN (to Rose): Can I drive you home? Make you a hot cup a coffee?

>ROSE: I think I'm okay now.

>VALJEAN: I'll take good care of you; don't worry.

Valjean puts his arm around Rose and she allows it.

Corky emerges from the crowd and glares at Valjean.

>CORKY: Valjean, where you been, boy? I need help with them snakes. And Darlynn.

Valjean removes his arm from around Rose.

>CORKY (to Rose): All the excitement's gettin' to you, ain't it? Well there's more to come. We still got a snake-huntin' date tomorrow, don't we?

>ROSE: I don't remember giving you a "yes" on that.

>CORKY: Well, if I ain't takin' you, I ain't takin' nobody. Come along now, boy.

Valjean helps Rose to her feet.

>VALJEAN: I'm gonna help Miss Rose to her car.

CORKY: Come along, now, Valjean. Darlynn's waitin' for you in the pickup. I need you to take her to the house. Goodnight, Miss Rose.

Corky snatches Valjean away from Rose and they disappear into the crowd.

CORKY: Don't you ever listen, boy? I want you to stay away from her, you hear me?

VALJEAN: I like her. And she likes me, too.

CORKY: Well I'm your daddy and you do what I say. You act quiet, but I know you got a big mouth on you.

VALJEAN: We don't talk about nothin'.

CORKY: See to it that you don't.

EXT. AUDITORIUM PARKING LOT - NIGHT
Rose slowly climbs into her car and takes a long, deep breath. She pulls out of the full parking lot and onto the highway.

EXT. HIGHWAY - NIGHT
Only a few cars are on the road; it seems like the entire town is still back at the auditorium. The stars are so bright you could reach out and touch them. Rose opens the moon roof and tries.

BOOM! The car veers dangerously from left to right. Loose gravel pummels the undercarriage of the car as she steers onto the shoulder. She coasts to a stop near the "Eden's Lair, Home of the World's Largest Rattlesnake Roundup" billboard.

INT./EXT. ROSE'S CAR - NIGHT

Paralyzed with fright, Rose takes quick, clipped breaths. She reaches over to the glove box and withdraws a flashlight. It glows a pale orange, flickers, and goes out. She grabs her purse, finds her phone, turns on the flashlight, and exits the car to investigate.

A carload of drunken Junior Snake Wranglers drives by, whooping and hollering. One of them throws a beer bottle at the billboard and makes a direct hit. Rose shields her face from flying glass.

Desperate and unnerved, Rose gets back in the car and locks the doors. The whooping and hollering fades into the distance.

EXT. SEEDY APARTMENT COMPLEX - NIGHT

Valjean's pickup pulls in. He drives past the open door of the game room where Chuck and Steve play poker and drink beer with other Junior Snake Wranglers. Chuck sees Valjean's truck, pokes Steve in the arm, and Steve turns to look. They shake their heads and start to laugh.

INT. VALJEAN'S APARTMENT - NIGHT

Valjean enters his apartment and flips on the light. His place is immaculate and tastefully decorated. A photograph of himself as a soldier sits on the mantle. A photo of his mother sits next to a photo of Valjean and Darlynn as seven and five-years-olds, respectively. A photo of Corky is conspicuously absent.

He walks into his bedroom. Something's not quite right.

    VALJEAN: Yep. Same ole routine.

He yanks back the covers, and coiled on the bed is a huge rattler.

VALJEAN: Slinky you gol durn critter. You peed on my pillow.

INT./EXT. ROSE'S CAR - NIGHT
To control her anxiety, Rose listens to a guided meditation podcast.

> RELAXATION VOICE (with a calming music bed): Close your eyes and focus on your breathing. Release all your thoughts. Breathe in, to the count of four, hold to the count of three, and exhale. Allow yourself to gently relax.

Headlights turned off, a truck slowly pulls up and stops several car-lengths behind Rose's car. The door shuts; leather shoes CRUNCH on loose gravel.

Click! A flashlight illuminates her face.

> KUNDOO: It's Kundoo, Miss Rose! I'm sorry to startle you. I was passing the other way and saw your car. May I be of assistance?

Bali, Kundoo's pet monkey, rides on his shoulders.

> ROSE: You scared the life out of me! Yes, please!

> KUNDOO: Let's have a look at that tire.

Rose exits the car. Kundoo finds the puncture.

> ROSE: I must have run over a rattlesnake.

> KUNDOO: Not unless it escaped from the coliseum. You won't be finding any rattlesnakes within fifty miles of Eden's

Lair.

Another carload of Junior Snake Wranglers drives by.

> ROSE: And you won't find any Junior Snake Wranglers anywhere else.

> KUNDOO: Let's get this thing off.

A few hundred yards away, a truck is parked on a rise. A shadowy figure watches Rose and Kundoo.

INT. VALJEAN'S BEDROOM - NIGHT
Valjean sits in a chair and shines his boots. His foot rests on the wooden box that contains Slinky. Valjean walks over to his closet. Everything is orderly and neat. He notices right away that his M16 is missing. He loses his composure and

INT. APARTMENT GAME ROOM - NIGHT
bursts through the door. Chuck and Steve are unruffled.

> VALJEAN: Okay, Chuck, where is it?

> CHUCK: Steve, your play.

> VALJEAN: You heard me.

> STEVE: Didn't you find ole Slinky yet?

> VALJEAN: I ain't talkin' about no snake.

> CHUCK: Well what are you talkin' about, pretty boy?

VALJEAN: My M16. It's gone.

CHUCK: You 'cusing us, Valjean? We've been sitting' here playin' poker all night tryin' to keep our minds offa that new Miss Snake Charmer.

VALJEAN: Which one of you took it?

CHUCK: Steve, you think he had this much trouble keepin' track of his gun in the Army? How the hell would we ever win a war with guys like him fightin' for us?

Valjean flies at Chuck.

INT. KUNDOO'S CAR - NIGHT

Rose and Kundoo drive down the highway. Rose breathes a heavy sigh.

KUNDOO: Something very terrifying has happened in your life, hasn't it?

ROSE: Is your intuition that good, or is it really obvious?

KUNDOO: One thing is clear. You have a deep wound that refuses to heal. It keeps you on guard, in a state of fear. If I may make a suggestion . . .

ROSE: Of course.

KUNDOO: I have something special that I brought to your country from India. After we drop off the tire, may I show it to you?

ROSE: I'd like that very much.

EXT./INT. KUNDOO'S HOUSE - NIGHT
Kundoo and Rose pull into his driveway.

Kundoo's wife CHANDRA greets them at the front door.

CHANDRA: Miss Rose, what a pleasure. Welcome to our home.

ROSE: Thank you, Chandra. Is Lakshmi asleep?

CHANDRA: She is. I'll go wake her.

ROSE: No, please don't. Just tell her "hello" for me in the morning.

(Kundoo talks to Chandra in Hindi; she takes Bali from him and excuses herself.)

CHANDRA: Enjoy! I call it Kundoo's Lair.

On their way to the back yard, Kundoo takes a small milk carton out of the refrigerator.

EXT. KUNDOO'S BACK YARD - NIGHT
Kundoo leads Rose to a large shed that resembles an Indian temple in miniature. He opens the doors to the shed to reveal

INT. SHED - NIGHT
an opulent display of Hindu imagery, lush fabrics, a beautiful rug on the floor, and silk toss pillows. The walls are festooned with garlands of plastic marigolds. The only pieces of furniture in the

room are a small sofa and a metal TV tray with an incense holder and a shallow dish. Kundoo places the milk carton on the tray. He closes the door and removes his shoes. Rose self-consciously removes hers.

>KUNDOO: Please sit here and do not move. It is very important that you remain perfectly still.

Kundoo lights a stick of incense. With measured, deliberate movements, he walks to a large woven basket and removes the lid. He joins Rose on the couch and withdraws a recorder-like instrument from under a cushion. He plays a simple, haunting melody.

A dark, thick form gracefully slides out of the basket. It stops a few feet from Kundoo and slowly grows as if it were a rope being pulled straight up. It reaches a height of six feet and extends its hood. Rose is paralyzed with fear. Kundoo gently sways back and forth. The cobra mimics his movements precisely.

Stifling a scream, Rose's hands clasp her mouth. The cobra reacts to the movement with a jerk.

>KUNDOO: Miss Rose, be still. The cobra will not harm you.

Kundoo coaxes the cobra to the ground. He curls up and is tranquil.

>KUNDOO: We have roundups in India, too, and they can be just as brutal. The snake charmers catch hundreds of them in the jungle and cut out their fangs. He is a rescue snake.

>ROSE: With or without fangs?

KUNDOO: I'll tell you after he's had his dinner. Please pour him some milk.

ROSE: I don't think I can.

KUNDOO: Look at your fear clearly and deeply. Have faith in yourself, and in him.

ROSE: Okay, I'll try.

KUNDOO: Move slowly.

ROSE: What do I do if *he* starts to move?

KUNDOO: He is waiting for you to bring his food. He knows he is a king and we are his subjects.

Rose rises from the couch as if she were moving through molasses. With great precision and caution, she puts one foot in front of the other and walks to the TV tray, never taking her eyes off the cobra.

Her hands shake as she tries to open the milk carton. Finally the flap "gives", and the force makes her drop the carton onto the tray. The metal dish tumbles to the floor, and reflexively, she snatches it up off the carpet.

The cobra rises up slightly from his coiled position, and after an interminable pause, lies back down.

ROSE: I. Can't. Do. This.

KUNDOO: He was only reacting to a change in the room's temperature. Cobras have no hearing.

ROSE: So the music?

KUNDOO: It's for tourists. The cobra would behave the same way without it. The milk, please?

Hands shaking even more, Rose pours a few ounces of milk into the dish. She lifts it from the tray and hands it to Kundoo.

KUNDOO: I've already eaten my dinner, thank you.

She puts it back down on the tray and begins to cry softly.

ROSE: I didn't know I was such a coward.

KUNDOO: Miss Rose, fearsome as a cobra is, he is also defined by what you perceive him to be. Say you're walking from your house to the car, it's dark, and a snake is lying in your path. It is really a rope, but you are frightened because you think it's a snake. When you realize that the truth is veiled by fear, you face your fears with courage. And in this moment, this is the simple truth: he wants his food.

She musters courage, picks up the dish of milk, and places it on the carpet a few feet from the cobra. He looks at her, then begins drinking the milk contentedly. Rose breaks out in nervous giggles.

EXT. ROSE'S HOUSE/INT. CAR - NIGHT
Rose's car pulls up to the house. Sitting on the steps to the front door is a large, covered basket.

She takes a deep breath and gets out of the car.

Grabbing a rake she's left in a flower bed, she approaches the basket. She lifts the lid with the rake and pushes it aside. (A beat) She takes a few steps toward the basket and leans over to look in. A greeting card sits on top of a bushel of apples.

>   ROSE (reading): Apples for the teacher. And to keep Dr. Ennis away. Hope you feel better. Valjean.

INT. ROSE'S BEDROOM/BATHROOM - NIGHT
Rose turns on the light. Bluster has pulled the covers off the bed and spread them around the room. His water dish is turned upside down. He appears at the bedroom door looking sheepish.

>   ROSE: Bluster! What's gotten into you?

She retreats into the bathroom, reappears with a towel, and mops up the mess. She makes the bed, smooths out the wrinkles, and folds down a corner.

She places the rose Sarah Jane gave her in a bud vase and sets one of Valjean's apples next to it. She picks the apple back up and considers it.

She returns the towel to the bathroom, washes the apple, and returns to the bedroom wearing a long-sleeved nightgown.
She secures the lock on the bedroom door.

Sitting on the bed, she takes a large bite out of the apple. Bluster begs for it; she takes it out of her mouth and gives it to him. She turns out the light and buries herself under the covers. (A beat) Her phone rings. Richard's name is displayed. She answers, tentatively.

ROSE: Richard?

INTERCUT - ROSE'S BEDROOM/RICHARD'S OFFICE - NIGHT

RICHARD: Hey.

In his small university office, Richard sits at a desk cluttered with books, papers, and objects collected from nature. A small parrot sits on top of his computer screen.

ROSE: Why are you calling at this hour?

RICHARD: I wanted to hear your voice. And I want to see you.

The bird SQUAWKS.

ROSE: You're still at school.

RICHARD: What can I do to fix things?

ROSE: Nothing comes to mind.

RICHARD: I've missed you every minute you've been gone. How can I earn your trust again?

Tears well up in his eyes.

ROSE: My life is settled now. Here. You'll have to figure yours out on your own.

RICHARD: Give me another chance, please.

ROSE: You already had your chance. And you can't understand. You've never been in a fight where everyone has a stick except you.

Richard can't find words. He manages to compose himself.

RICHARD: The department head is sending me to Eden's Lair tomorrow to lead a protest. (A beat) I need to talk to you. Hold you. If you'll let me.

ROSE: Richard, stay home. The Roundup is a three-ring circus. And I can't handle seeing you right now.

RICHARD: I want to make things right with us. And I want to be there for you, always.

ROSE: Are you coming for me, or for work? (She begins to cry.) I never thought that settling back into myself would be so difficult.

RICHARD: You're not settling in, you're running away.

ROSE: It happened to me, not you. I'm hanging up now. Bye.

Rose, restless, gets out of bed and walks to the window. Forks of lightning discharge in the distance. Thunder rolls toward her like a giant tumbleweed.

Rose tosses and turns in bed. Rain pelts the window.

BEGIN DREAM SEQUENCE

The old oak tree in the town square. It begins to vibrate slightly as milk percolates up from underneath its gnarled roots. The roots turn into snakes that slither off in all directions. The talismans on the tree drop off into the milk and float away.

The milk becomes a raging river. Rose stands on the banks watching. A gigantic cobra rises straight up out of the river and spreads its hood. A small, unmanned wooden raft floats down the river and stops directly in front of her. Kundoo stands on the opposite shore with Bali on his shoulder.

> KUNDOO: You must cross the river. Hurry!

Eden's Lair's mothers crowd her with their baby carriages and force her onto the raft. One of the mothers ties Rose's hair with a black ribbon. Another hands her a pole. The raft launches into the river and the cobra disappears beneath its surface.

Kundoo urges her on. No matter how hard Rose poles, the shore recedes more and more. The river picks up speed, and the raft twists and turns violently. She loses her pole, lies down, and grabs an edge.

All of a sudden Darlynn materializes. The raft's planks turn into writhing snakes that entangle Rose and Darlynn. The snakes tear their clothes off, and the two women open their mouths to scream but nothing comes out.

The cobra rises out of the water again and spreads its hood. It stares menacingly at Rose and Darlynn.

DARLYNN: We didn't do nothin'!

ROSE: Kundoo, help us!

END OF DREAM SEQUENCE

Rose awakens with a start. The sheets are twisted around her body. She extricates herself and goes to the bathroom for a drink of water. Her phone RINGS. She returns to the bedroom. It's 3 a.m. She doesn't recognize the number.

INTERCUT BAR/BEDROOM - NIGHT

Corky hands a MAN in a phone booth a glass of beer. The man takes a swig then licks his lips.

Rose decides to take the call.

ROSE: Richard?

The man whispers into the receiver.

MAN: There's a snake in your bed. It's long and hard and wants to crawl up inside you.

Rose gasps and disconnects the call. She tentatively walks around to the other side of the bed.

She yanks back the sheets. Nothing. She curls up in a rocking chair near the window and collapses into sobs.

INT. DARLYNN'S BEDROOM - EARLY MORNING
A soft light filters through the second storey window. Shadows of leaves dance across Darlynn's peaceful face and silk nightgown.

Corky opens the door and silently walks in, wearing nothing but boxer shorts. With the greatest care, so as not to wake her, he pulls the covers down and slides in beside her.

INT. CONVENIENCE STORE – EARLY MORNING
Carrying a paper bag, Rose enters the store.

> KUNDOO: Good morning, Miss Rose. Going snake hunting today?

> ROSE: Yes. And I'd like to return this.

She pulls the snake bite kit out of the bag and lays it on the counter. Kundoo slides it toward himself.

> KUNDOO: Just a minute, please.

Kundoo opens a drawer under the counter and pulls something out.

> KUNDOO: Miss Rose, I want you to have this.

Kundoo hands her a mysterious vial strung on a silk cord necklace.

> ROSE: What is it?

> KUNDOO: A special potion from India. Keep the vial around your neck and hope you never need to use it.

Rose tentatively puts on the necklace.

>   ROSE: For snakebite?

>   KUNDOO: I'm wearing one myself.

Kundoo pulls an identical necklace and vial out from under his shirt.

>   KUNDOO: God forbid you ever have to use it.

Kundoo reaches into his pocket. He opens up his hand. A 5.56-millimeter bullet—about the size of an AA battery—from an M16 rifle sits in his palm.

>   KUNDOO: And this is what caused your flat, Miss Rose. It doesn't pay to be out on the road late at night.

With terror in her eyes, Rose takes the bullet out of Kundoo's hand. She fingers the bullet nervously, then puts it in her purse.

>   ROSE: Do you think it was an accident?

>   KUNDOO: Of course. I know how much beer the population consumes during this weekend. Why would you think otherwise?

EXT. EDEN'S LAIR BAPTIST CHURCH - EARLY MORNING
The townspeople file into church. An USHER hands out programs.

INT. CHURCH - EARLY MORNING

Rose sits next to one of her students. Solemn organ music plays as the PREACHER takes his place at the pulpit. A large stained-glass window of St. George slaying the dragon is in the b.g.

> PREACHER: And the Lord God said unto the woman, what is this that thou hast done? And the woman said, the serpent beguiled me, and I did eat.

Valjean rushes in; he looks around for Rose. He tiptoes up the aisle, enters the pew where she sits, and squeezes in next to her. They exchange flirtatious smiles. She notices the bruise on his cheek and a long gash under his eye, and looks puzzled.

> PREACHER: And the Lord God said unto the serpent, thou art cursed above all the cattle in the field; upon thy belly shalt thou go, and dust shalt thou eat all the days of thy life. And I will put enmity between thee and the woman, and between thy seed and her seed; she shall bruise thy head, and thou shalt bruise her heel.

Valjean lightly touches his bruise. He glances at Rose's daintily crossed ankles.

> PREACHER: So the Lord God drove out Adam and Eve, and he placed at the east of the garden of Eden, cherubims, and a flaming sword which turned every which way, to keep the way of the Tree of Life.

Corky appears at the back of the room and stands with his hands folded in front of his crotch. The Preacher looks up and acknowledges Corky with a nod.

PREACHER: Welcome, friends, to the most important sermon of the year, not counting Christmas and Easter, of course.

Knowing laughter from the congregation.

PREACHER: Today is Rattlesnake Roundup Sunday, when we remember the words of Genesis, chapter three, verses one through twenty-four. Remember these words and live by these words. Why? Because they were set down by the Lord God himself, and we have a covenant with the Lord that must not be broken. A covenant that says, destroy the beast that first destroyed us.

Rose rolls her eyes and nervously fans her face with the church program.

PREACHER: And the woman said unto the serpent, we may eat of the fruit of the trees of the garden, but of the fruit of the tree in the midst of the garden, God hath said, Ye shall not eat of it, neither shall you touch it, lest you die. And the serpent said unto the woman, ye shall not surely die; for God doth know that in the day ye eat thereof, then your eyes shall be opened, and ye shall be as gods, knowing good and evil.

The congregation responds with affirmations.

PREACHER: Friends, the serpent stole our immortality. He stole our innocence; he stole our happiness. He made us feel shame for our bodies. He made us want to hide from the Lord.

Rose shifts restlessly in her seat. Valjean looks at her, but she does not return his gaze.

> PREACHER: And I say to you today, as it was put forth in the Bible over two thousand years ago; let the destroyer of all moral values, the hellion incarnate, eat dust all the days of his life.

The congregation responds with cheers. Disgusted, Rose makes a hasty retreat. Valjean follows after her.

EXT. CHURCH - EARLY MORNING
Rose breaks into a fast walk as she heads for her car. Valjean catches up with her as she unlocks the door.

> VALJEAN: Miss Rose, wait! I think he's full of bull, too. He's playing to his audience. Doin' his job.

> ROSE: It's one thing to rid Eden's Lair of a few inconvenient snakes, but it's another to encourage a wholesale massacre of innocent animals.

Corky strolls up.

> CORKY: Innocent? In 1998, a huge rattler bit Mrs. Jones's little boy in his own back yard. That little boy died, Miss Rose. So who was the innocent? Not the damn snake.

> ROSE: Mr. Dodds, we don't kill snakes to fulfill some Biblical injunction. The boy and the snake; they're both innocent. What happened is called being at the wrong place at the wrong time.

Rose has a new understanding of her own tragedy back in Dallas.

> ROSE: It's a matter of luck. Or the absence of it. (A beat) This snake-butchering hysteria is way out of proportion to any real

danger. Lightning strikes cause more injuries than snakes.

CORKY: That's the book-learnin' part of you talkin' again. That's the problem with you schoolteachers. You talk big in the classroom, but drag you out into the real world and what you think you know ain't the truth at all.

ROSE: What I read is written by authorities on their subjects. PhDs.

CORKY: I'm just sayin' thays some things out there you can't get the knowledge of from some ole college doctor, but you can from a durn U-Haul man from Eden's Lair, Texas. So are you goin' snake huntin' with me this afternoon or not? If you're not, you're givin' up your chance to prove me wrong.

ROSE: Yes, I am. Pick me up in an hour?

CORKY: Yes, mam.

Rose gets into her car and speeds away, kicking dust into Valjean and Corky's faces.

INT. ROSE'S BEDROOM/BATHROOM/THE STAIRWAY - MID MORNING

Rose puts on a pair of long pants. She vacillates between tennis shoes and knee-high boots. She chooses the knee-highs.

She enters the bathroom when the sound of the front door CREAKING downstairs makes her stop dead in her tracks. Bluster, sleeping at the foot of her bed, awakens with a start and emits a low growl.

ROSE: Stay, boy.

She approaches the stairway for a look and pauses to listen. Nothing seems out of the ordinary. She returns to the bathroom and brushes her hair.

She pats Bluster on the head.

ROSE: I'm going to have to lock you in again, Bluster. We've got a guest coming over. Be a good boy and don't tear everything up.

She sprints down the stairway, bounds into the kitchen,

INT. ROSE'S KITCHEN - MID MORNING
and stops so suddenly she nearly falls on her face. A violent tremor travels through her body.

There in the middle of the floor is a huge rattlesnake staring up at the doves. The doves are frantic; the snake is coiled and flicking its tongue.

The vial given her by Kundoo sits on the kitchen table, out of reach.

She fights the impulse to run. She scoots a trash can between herself and the snake. The snake looks quickly in the direction of the sound. The trash can teeters and crashes to the floor. Bluster starts to BARK upstairs. The snake retreats to a corner of the kitchen.

She moves slowly toward a closet and retrieves a broom. She opens the screen door leading out of the kitchen, her eyes never leaving the snake. She props the door open with a flowerpot.

With the brush-end of the broom, she coaxes the snake out of its corner. The frightened snake coils and strikes. Rose loses control and screams.

Corky appears: a snake hook-wielding Indiana Jones.

> CORKY: Don't move, Miss Rose, don't move. Do what Corky tells you. Hand me the broom. Now back up slowly, slowly, easy, easy.

Corky provokes the snake with the broom and the snake strikes.

> ROSE: Why'd you do that? You're scaring him.

> CORKY: I'm tryin' to git him out the door without us gittin' bit. Why don't you go upstairs and git that dog to shut up?

> ROSE: Just use your snake hook and pick him up.

> CORKY: It ain't that easy. You've gotta out-manipulate him. Git him into position so you *can* pick him up. I ain't playin' no games here.

The snake tries to retreat into the closet. Corky slams the door shut with the broom before it can get in.

> ROSE: You almost crushed its head!

> CORKY: Oh, the poor little ole rattlesnake. Miss Rose, when are you gonna learn there ain't no such thing as a poor little ole

rattlesnake?

ROSE: Give me the hook.

CORKY: What??

ROSE: Give me the hook!

CORKY: Are you sure you don't want to just grab him with your bare hands?

Rose takes the hook from Corky and gently picks up the snake.

ROSE: Step aside, please.

EXT. ROSE'S BACK YARD - MID MORNING
Rose carefully walks down the stairs and across the yard to the back fence. Corky watches from the open screen door. She gently places the snake in the grass, releases it, and breaks out in a slow run for the house.

Corky moves the flowerpot that's holding the screen door open, closes the door, and holds it closed so she can't get back in.

ROSE: Okay, let me back in my house.

CORKY: Miss Rose, I'm mighty impressed with that nice piece of snake wranglin'.

Rose tugs on the handle.

ROSE: Let me in!

CORKY: Here he comes! You ain't pregnant, are you?

Corky releases the door, throwing Rose back on her rear. A little panicky, she looks in the direction of the snake. Corky steps outside and helps her stand up.

ROSE (suspiciously): I wonder how he got into the kitchen? I've been burning old shoes in the oven to keep the snakes away.

CORKY: Where'd you hear about doin' that?

ROSE: Book learnin'.

Rose brushes off the seat of her pants as she enters the kitchen. Corky watches with interest.

CORKY: I think you liked wranglin' that snake. You're lookin' mighty purdy right now. 'Scuse me a minute.

EXT. CORKY'S TRUCK/VALJEAN'S APARTMENT - MID MORNING

Corky removes a large burlap snake sack from the front seat and tosses it into the back of the truck. He calls Valjean on his cell.

CORKY: Son, get over here to Miss Rose's and find Slinky. He done escaped into the field behind her house.

Wearing nothing but boxers, Valjean irons a nice dress shirt.

VALJEAN: What?? Okay, Corky. (to himself) What the hell have you done?

INT. ROSE'S KITCHEN - MID MORNING
Rose smells her hands then washes them vigorously. She checks the doves to make sure they're all right. She puts on the necklace with the vial.

Corky returns with a pair of chaps and slaps them down on the kitchen table.

> CORKY: I brought these for you to wear on our snake hunt. For extra protection.

> ROSE: Thank you, that was very thoughtful. But do I have to take everything else off?

Corky glares at Rose.

INT. DARLYNN'S BEDROOM - MID MORNING
Darlynn slips out of bed and puts on her robe. She walks to the door, turns the knob—it's locked. She tries the door again. Howling like a trapped animal, she kicks the door and pounds it with her fists.

She grabs her phone. There's a text from Corky: "This is for your own good. You know you don't have no business being at the Roundup. See you tonight."

Darlynn resists the urge to tear the room apart and dissolves into tears instead.

INT. DODD'S U-HAUL - MID MORNING
Corky and Rose walk in. A group of SNAKE HUNTERS and Junior Snake Wranglers greets Corky. The front room looks like an army general's headquarters: a topographical map placed on a

large table is marked with red push pins showing the locations of the biggest snake dens; gas canisters and other snake hunting equipment is lined up in neat rows.

Corky's office is behind the counter. A sign on the door to his office reads: "Private: Authorized Personnel Only." Underneath it someone has scrawled, "If Corky's rattlin' his tail, STOP. Back up slow."

Chuck and Steve stand at a whiteboard updating the tally of pounds of snakes captured. The whiteboard shows statistics from the last three rattlesnake roundups.

>CORKY: Mornin', boys. Y'all look dragged out and it ain't even ten o'clock yet.

>STEVE: Most of us has been here since seven.

>CORKY: What the hell for? Y'all know huntin' ain't no good before ten-thirty, eleven. I take it these canisters are still empty, else y'all wouldn't be smokin' like a gol durn chimney?

Several hunters spring into action, grab their canisters, and walk out the door with them.

>CORKY: This here's Miss Rose, the fourth-grade teacher down at the elementary school.

>ROSE: Nice to meet all of you.

>CORKY: Y'all keep her company. I got to find that boy o' mine.

Corky pulls out his phone and walks outside.

> STEVE: So what kinda interest you got in snake huntin'? Most women won't even step foot inside Corky's U-Haul.
>
> ROSE: Curiosity, that's all. It's the teacher in me.
>
> CHUCK: We ain't never had no woman go along on a snake hunt before. We'll have to mind our manners, boys. Leave the six-packs behind.
>
> ROSE: Don't do anything differently on my account.
>
> CHUCK: Just make sure you don't get too close to that big den we're huntin' at. A snake might wrap its tail 'round your leg and drag you in.
>
> STEVE: If Corky don't do it first.

Chuck glares at Steve, and the group laughs to diffuse Steve's gaffe.

EXT. DODD'S U-HAUL - MID MORNING
Valjean pulls up in his truck, kicking up dust, and skids to a stop. Corky is supremely vexed.

> CORKY: Where you been, boy? Did you find Slinky?
>
> VALJEAN: I sent Toby out to look for him. What were you doing at Miss Rose's?

CORKY: Damn! Slinky's the last of the really big ones. Is the snake sacks in the den?

VALJEAN: Chuck took care of it early this morning. WHAT WERE YOU DOING AT HER HOUSE?

CORKY: It's gotta wait, boy. Adam and Jason are gonna meet the environ-meddle-ists. They're supposed to arrive any minute, and I wanna be outta here.

INT. DODD'S U-HAUL - MID MORNING

ROSE: What do you do with the snakes once you catch them?

CHUCK: We skin 'em, cook 'em, and the Junior Wranglers sell the hides to make belts and key chains and hatbands, things like that. Then we give the money to charity.

STEVE: But first we milk 'em. Hang their fangs over a glass and let that yeller jism come streamin' out.

CHUCK: Watch your mouth, Steve! You're talkin' to a lady, not Corky.

STEVE: Then we donate it for medical research, ain't that right, Chuck?

Steve scoops up a handful of papers off the counter.

STEVE: We got a bunch of letters here thankin' us for it. Even from that disease place in Atlanta, Georgia.

Steve accidentally drops one of the letters. It falls at Rose's feet, and she stoops to pick it up.

> ROSE: "Highly contaminated" doesn't sound very complimentary.

As she hands the letter back to Steve, Corky bursts through the door and sees Steve with the letters. He yanks them out of his hand and stuffs them underneath the counter.

> CORKY: Miss Rose, it ain't what you think. We had a storage issue with one of our batches and we issued a recall. Our communication done crossed in the mail.

Rose doesn't buy it.

> CORKY: Steve and Chuck, go help Valjean load the truck.

ULYSSES S. PIERCE, a tall, young, African American greenhorn Texas Ranger, walks through the door.

> CORKY: Miss Rose, this here's Mr. Ulysses S. Pierce.

> ULYSSES: Pleased to meet you.

> CORKY: He's here to make sure we kill the rattlesnake right. Some environ-meddle-ist group in Dallas is trying to close us down. Claim we kill the rattlesnake wrong.

> ULYSSES (an aside to Rose): This is my first assignment.

ROSE: He probably wants to make sure the animals aren't mistreated or over-harvested.

CORKY: Over-harvested? We ain't talkin' no green beans, Miss Rose. You know how many pounds of rattlesnakes we "harvest" every year?

Corky walks over to the whiteboard.

CORKY: Last year, over 30,000 pounds. The year before that, 28,000. And this year we expect over 40,000 pounds of snakes. Them numbers are increasin', not decreasin'. Hell, that's four pounds of snakes for every man, woman, and child in Eden's Lair!

Valjean appears. Rose registers the fury in his face.

VALJEAN: Ready, Corky.

Corky hands a map to Jason, who's manning the counter.

CORKY: Jason, give the environ-meddle-ists this here map to the den. I wouldn't want 'em to git lost.

EXT. THE PLAINS - LATE MORNING
Lead by Chuck, a caravan of trucks pulling U-Hauls travels down a dusty road. A chorus of WHOOPING AND HOLLERING echoes across the plains. Corky brings up the rear.

INT. CORKY'S TRUCK - LATE MORNING
Corky, Rose, and Ulysses ride in the front seat. Valjean is relegated to the truck bed, sitting among the canisters, snake sacks, and

other snake hunting equipment.

CORKY: Ever been on a snake hunt, Mr. Pierce?

ULYSSES: Only once, when I was a boy. A snake bit my grandmother, and my dad organized a posse of neighbors to find it and kill it. They ended up with about twenty snakes and killed every last one of them. I remember the pile of dead snakes out by the barn, and hundreds of those big green flies buzzing around it. Within a couple of weeks of that, there were lots and lots of rats. My grandmother got bitten by one of them, too.

EXT. RATTLESNAKE DEN - LATE MORNING
The trucks line up and the hunters leap out. They don their protective gear: chaps, elbow-high leather gloves, leather vests. They mount gas masks on top of their heads.

INT. CORKY'S TRUCK - LATE MORNING
Corky sees Chuck, Earl Scrogie, and other hunters sneaking swallows from their beers.

CORKY: 'Scuse me a second. Y'all stay here.

EXT. RATTLESNAKE DEN - LATE MORNING
Corky storms up to the group.

CORKY: I said no drinkin', you understand? We're bein' scrutinized by the law and by y'all's daughter's teacher. So lay off.

CHUCK: This ain't no hunt; this is show and tell.

CORKY: I ain't happy about it neither. But just lay off for now. You can make up for it tonight.

Corky returns to Rose and Ulysses.

CORKY: Okay, y'all. It's time. Mr. Pierce and me'll go on over to the den. (to Rose) Wait here 'till I give the signal. And don't forget them chaps.

She walks to the back of the truck to get the chaps. Valjean, wearing his crisply ironed shirt and best cowboy hat, is off-loading the truck. He seizes the opportunity to talk to Rose.

VALJEAN: Miss Rose, I fixed the hinges on your tornado shelter. It looks like we might get a granddaddy of a storm tonight.

Thunderclouds are building in the distance.

Rose is suspicious.

ROSE: You were at my house? When?

VALJEAN: I was drivin' by about twenty minutes ago.

(The timing is off. Valjean couldn't have put the snake in her kitchen.)

ROSE: Thanks, Valjean, but I hope I never have to see the inside of a tornado shelter.

VALJEAN: Miss Rose, when we start huntin', you'll be sure and stand way back out of the way, won't you? So you don't get bit?

ROSE: Unless they come flying out, I don't think there'll be a problem.

Rose smiles and lets Valjean take her hand.

VALJEAN: It's just that I wouldn't want nothin' to happen to you. You know when we were sittin' in my pickup at the edge of the cliff, and I told you how I felt about bein' here in Eden's Lair? How I don't fit in? This is the first time in my life that everyday things has had some magic. Like I'm really participatin', not just watchin'.

Valjean moves in a little closer.

VALJEAN: It's you, Rose; you're what's made the difference.

Valjean has dropped the "Miss" from her name, and she's taken aback.

ROSE: Funny—I try not to notice those everyday things as much. I liked life a lot better when I could take them for granted.

VALJEAN: What would make you feel awright again?

ROSE: Living in a simple, quiet little place. Untouched by the ugly things that find you in a big city. Someplace where I can get back what Dallas took away.

VALJEAN: Is it something I could give you? That would make you happy? I'd sure like to try.

She lowers her gaze and is silent. Tears roll down her cheeks.

>   VALJEAN: I understand. I mean about gettin' away. I really do.

She looks into Valjean's face, searching for answers.

>   ROSE: How do you know who to trust?
>
>   VALJEAN: You know he'd never betray you. That he has your interests at heart more than his own. That his greatest gift is the truth, even if it hurts.
>
>   ROSE: I trust you, Valjean. And I never thought I'd trust anyone ever again.

Valjean tentatively pulls Rose toward him and holds her close, but a surge of guilt preempts the possibility of a kiss, which they both want more than anything.

>   VALJEAN: You've made me so happy, Rose. But I need to tell you some things, too.

Valjean's face clouds over.

Corky sees the two of them and snaps to what's going on.

>   CORKY: Valjean! Bring me a canister and one of them pocket mirrors.

Valjean sighs with exasperation.

VALJEAN: Okay, Corky!

CORKY: And tell Miss Rose it's okay to proceed.

VALJEAN: Can I take you to supper tonight? Please say yes.

ROSE: I'd love to. I *need* to.

A slow smile spreads across his face. His hat flies off as he sprints in Corky's direction. Rose picks it up.

ROSE: Your hat!

VALJEAN: Keep it for me; I'll get it later!

Huge speakers sit in the back of one of the trucks. A hunter inserts a CD in the truck's player and presses play. It's "Ride of the Valkyries".

CORKY: I love the smell of gasoline in the morning.

A local TV crew arrives on the scene, in a helicopter. It hovers near the den, churning up an enormous amount of dust.

Steve and Chuck slip into the den, grab several burlap bags full of snakes that were hidden from view, and empty them near the mouth of the den.

The helicopter lands, and a camera crew emerges with Bob—the Miss Snake Charmer M.C.—dressed in his costume suit of armor and ready to cover the event.

Rose grabs her purse from the truck, removes a bandana, and covers her nose and mouth. She decides to leave the chaps behind, and with her purse and Valjean's hat walks up the small rise to the embankment, which makes a semi-circle around the den.

Sounds of frenzied activity emanate from the den. Rose is totally unprepared for what she sees. The dust settles to reveal an ominous, gaping hole in a huge rock outcropping. The den looks like the entrance to hell.

Ulysses sits at the edge of the embankment. Rose joins him.

Corky, Valjean, the hunters, and their equipment are assembled at the mouth of the den. Snake sacks and large metal trash cans are ready to receive the snakes.

Rose and Valjean lock eyes. She puts on his hat, lowers the bandana, and smiles.

The film crew is ready. Bob gives Corky a "we're rolling" sign, and Corky hands Steve a mirror.

>   CORKY: Steve, you've got the mirror, so lead the way. Y'all put on your gas masks!

The Snake Wranglers comply. Chuck pumps gasoline into the den. Steve moves cautiously around the mouth of the den, reflecting light inside with his mirror.

>   ROSE: Who sent you here, Mr. Pierce?

>   ULYSSES: State headquarters in Austin. Another group of Rangers is coming in from Lubbock. The environmental issue

is only part of it. Local law's being paid off.

ROSE: Why?

ULYSSES: That's what I'm here to find out.

Corky removes his gas mask, picks up a megaphone, and flips the switch. He plays to Rose and Ulysses.

CORKY: What's really handy to have along on a snake hunt is a little ole pocket mirror like Steve's got. What it does is reflect light back up in the den, and if the light hits the snake just right, his scales light right up.

ULYSSES: I took a first aid refresher course not too long ago, and guess what? Snake bite is so rare these days that it's been dropped from the training.

ROSE: Don't tell that to the Junior Snake Wranglers.

CORKY: The gas in these here canisters is used for extractin' the rattler. But unless we spot something down in the den, we don't use no gas. We're real environ-meddle. But one time we skeet gas in a hole and a skunk come out first. You can imagine what kind of gas he put out on us!

Valjean rolls his eyes and shakes his head.

Steve feeds the gas line from the canister into the den, and Chuck pumps the gas.

CORKY: What Steve and Chuck are going to do now is back out of the den real slow, squirtin' gas all the way.

Corky keeps the megaphone close to his mouth so Rose and Ulysses can hear his running commentary. Bob directs the camera crew.

CORKY (to Steve): Just back out real slow with it, Steve. Make sure you git plenty around the mouth.

Steve pulls the gas line out of the den and removes his gas mask.

CORKY: Steve, why don't you go on in there and see if they haven't started comin' out yet. Watch his back, Chuck, watch his back.

Steve gets down on his hands and knees. Chuck hands him a snake hook.

Corky produces an M16 rifle. Valjean does a double take. It's his missing firearm.

CORKY: Valjean's gonna stand by with his Army-issue M16, just as a protective measure. (to Valjean) Load your rifle, son.

Of course, this is overkill and just for show.

Rose rummages in her purse for the bullet that Kundoo gave her.

ROSE: Mr. Pierce, could this bullet have come from that gun?

ULYSSES: Sure could have. It's the right size.

Rose is paralyzed with fear and disbelief. She removes Valjean's hat.

STEVE: They've started coming out.

CORKY: Okay, bring 'em on out. Be careful with 'em. Be careful.

Steve pulls out one snake after another.

CORKY: Let ole Chucker handle 'em now. Okay, coil it up right there. Let him air out a little.

Several other hunters step forward to help Chuck with the massive number of snakes that Steve delivers from the den. The hunt is orderly and in control.

CORKY: Good lord, look at all them snakes! Keep roundin' 'em up. Watch his back, Chuck, watch his back. Take that mirror again, Steve. I'll bet there's a biggun in there. He'll probably be the last one to come out.

The hunters carefully place the snakes into the trash cans and the sacks.

STEVE: I got the granddaddy here!

CORKY: Got a biggun? That's just what I was thinking. Good Lord! Now he is fat, he is fat!

Steve and Chuck hold Slinky horizontally so that Rose and Ulysses can appreciate his length.

CORKY: Mr. Pierce, would you like to come down and put him in this here snake sack?

ULYSSES: No, y'all go on ahead.

ROSE: Go on, Mr. Pierce. If I did it, so can you.

ULYSSES: You've done this before?

ROSE: I found one in my kitchen this morning, just about that size. The big difference is you've got the area's finest snake wranglers helping you.

ULYSSES: Well, I can't be shown up now, can I? And miss the opportunity to be on local news?

Ulysses joins the group below.

CORKY: Okay, Mr. Pierce. May I call you Ulysses?

ULYSSES: Okay by me.

CORKY: Okay, Ulysses. Come stand here by me and listen real careful. Steve's gonna hand you the tail-end first, then Chucker's gonna show you where to hold the head.

ULYSSES: I don't know about this.

CORKY: Don't worry, I'm right here. I ain't gonna let nothin' happen to you. And these boys has all done this before. It's our little initiation. A way of welcomin' you to the club.

ULYSSES: Okay, but let me get my gloves.

CORKY: Gloves ain't gonna help you no how. And he's gittin' impatient. He ain't no kitty-cat that's gonna lay in your arms and purr.

Slinky starts to squirm.

CORKY: Come on. I'll talk you through it.

Ulysses plants himself firmly on the ground, like a golf pro preparing his swing.

CORKY: Now. Take his body away from Steve.

Ulysses does what he's told. He shudders as he takes hold of the snake's body.

ULYSSES: He's not slimy!

CORKY: That's right! Snakes is rough, he ain't no garden slug.

ULYSSES: He's strong, too!

Slinky is getting distressed.

CORKY: He's gittin' agitated. We better move fast. Valjean, put that gun down and bring the sack closer. Ulysses, you stand real still. And Miss Rose, would you mind watchin' the den in case any more come out?

ROSE: You'll be the first to know.

CORKY: Okay, you ready?

ULYSSES: Ready as I'll ever be.

CORKY: Now, when Chuck releases his grip, you gotta slip your fingers in there and grab him by the back of the head, okay?

ULYSSES: What if he turns his head around?

CORKY: I swear, where do these ideas come from? We ain't got no snappin' turtle here neither. Ready, Chuck?

CHUCK: Yes, sir!

Chuck releases Slinky's head.

CORKY: GO!

Ulysses grabs the snake's head. The snake begins to writhe violently. Ulysses is panicky.

CORKY: You're okay, you're okay. Loosen your grip a little. Okay, hold that sack open, boys. Ulysses, walk over here away from everybody.

Ulysses and the sack holders follow Corky.

CORKY: Now, when I tell you, I want you to drop him. And get away from him real quick. Okay?

ULYSSES: Roger that.

CORKY: Ready?

Ulysses nods.

CORKY: NOW!

Slinky drops directly into the sack. Everyone applauds Ulysses, and Corky shakes his hand vigorously. Some of the snake hunters slap him on the rear end as if he'd just scored the winning touchdown.

Bob joins the group, flips up the helmet's visor, and shakes Ulysses's hand.

BOB: Congratulations, now you're an official Eden's Lair snake wrangler. Ulysses, your hand's kinda clammy. You're not going into shock, are you?

ULYSSES: No, but I didn't know if I was going to pass out or have a heart attack first.

BOB: The boys back in Austin'll be mighty proud. Are you gonna help Corky put some of 'em back now?

ULYSSES: Back in the den?

CORKY: Yep. We don't take no more out than's necessary. Don't want to upset the delicate balance of nature. If we take out every last one of 'em, we don't have nothin' to hunt next year. We're just trying to control the species.

ULYSSES: I'll let you take over from here.

> CORKY: Steve, Chuck, take five or six of them snakes out of that trash can and make sure they's all right afore you let 'em go. Let go of that granddaddy snake last.
>
> STEVE AND CHUCK: Yes, sir, Corky.

Bob and the camera crew film Chuck returning some of the snakes to the den.

Ulysses and Rose walk back to Corky's truck.

> ULYSSES: So far, so good. I don't see anything wrong with what they're doing.
>
> ROSE: At least they don't charge admission. They were putting on a show for us, Mr. Pierce.
>
> ULYSSES: Well, I see no harm in it. The animal rights groups may be over-reacting. Notice that not even one of them bothered to come see it for themselves?
>
> ROSE: Yes, I noticed.

INTERCUT - EXT. THE PLAINS - DAY
The caravan of animal rights protesters drives down a dirt road. Richard, Rose's husband, is in the lead. He stops, gets out of his car, and looks at the make-shift map provided him by Adam back at the U-Haul store. They're lost. He's exasperated.

BACK TO SCENE
Valjean climbs up the embankment.

VALJEAN: Corky says go ahead and take his truck back to the shop. We need to clean up the area a little 'fore we leave.

Valjean tosses Ulysses the keys.

ULYSSES: Be sure to thank your dad for us.

ROSE: Mr. Pierce, would you excuse me for a moment?

ULYSSES: Sure. Meet you at the truck.

Ulysses heads for the truck.

Rose hands Valjean his hat. She opens her other hand, the one holding the bullet.

ROSE: Is this yours, too?

VALJEAN: Where'd you get this?

ROSE: Out of my tire. Is this what you wanted to tell me?

Corky sees Valjean and Rose. He raises his megaphone.

CORKY: Valjean!

VALJEAN: No! It's not what you think.

CORKY: Come on back down here, boy!

VALJEAN: I'm not like them. That's what I've been trying to tell you. It's Corky, he's . . .

ROSE: How do you explain this?

CORKY: VALJEAN!!!

Valjean slides down the embankment. He looks back at Rose.

VALJEAN: Please trust me! Are we still on for supper?

Rose turns and storms off.

CORKY: She had enough of your bullshit? Well, so have I. Wait 'till they're out of sight, then git them snakes outta there. Make sure Slinky don't get away again. And hurry it up, I gotta git back to the coliseum.

Rose and Ulysses drive off into the distance.

EXT. COLISEUM - LATE AFTERNOON
While Richard and his group are lost somewhere on the plains, another faction of the protestors pickets the Roundup. Toby guards the closed entrance.

Rose and Ulysses pull into the parking lot in Corky's truck. Rose scans the crowd for Richard.

Corky and Valjean pull up.

CORKY: God damn environ-meddle-ists. The Sheriff was supposed to care of this. Demonstratin' is illegal.

VALJEAN: No, it ain't.

CORKY: Valjean, why don't you never say the right thing? Sometimes I can't believe you're Corky Dodds's son. And that sister of yours . . . If you don't straighten up, next year you're gonna find yourself in a clown costume, whompin' rattlers upside the head with a foam hatchet.

Now that Rose has lost her trust in Valjean, his humiliation overrides his anger at Corky. He wants Corky's respect back.

CORKY: Git your tail outta the truck and go find Chuck.

VALJEAN: What do you need, Dad? I can do it.

CORKY: Go find Chuck!

VALJEAN: Yes, sir.

Valjean pushes his way through the crowd to the coliseum entrance.

VALJEAN: Let me through, Toby.

Several people try to push through with Valjean, but Toby tosses them back.

Rose meanders through the crowd.

ROSE: Richard! Richard!

He's nowhere in sight.

WOMAN PICKETER: Are you looking for Dr. McGrath from the University?

ROSE: Yes, where is he?

WOMAN PICKETER: He's with another group that's supposed to be here, too.

MAN PICKETER: He'd better show up soon, or he'll miss all the fun.

ROSE (to herself): Never around when you need him.

INT. COLISEUM - LATE AFTERNOON
Valjean finds Chuck. He's flirting with Suzie Scrogie, who's wearing a pretty party dress and her Miss Snake Charmer banner.

VALJEAN: Corky wants you out front.

CHUCK: Can't you see I'm busy, pretty boy?

VALJEAN: It's an emergency, Chuck.

CHUCK: Then why don't you take care of it? Or did you lose your gun again?

Valjean looks like he might hit Chuck, but because Suzie is present, he restrains himself. Corky storms up in a rage.

CORKY: Valjean Dodds, I can't count on you for nothin'! Go on home, you sonofabitch. GIT!

Barely restraining his fury, Valjean leaves.

EXT. COLISEUM - LATE AFTERNOON
Ominous storm clouds frame the coliseum. The double doors open, and a pickup backs up into the crowd. Corky's standing on the tail gate. Junior Snake Wranglers rush to close the doors before the crowd can get it. A JSW hands Corky his megaphone.

Rose and Ulysses are among the crowd.

>   CORKY: Ladies and gentlemen. Welcome to the 25th Annual Eden's Lair Rattlesnake Roundup. Now, I understand that some of y'all are a little upset about what y'all think we do here.

>   MAN PICKETER (sarcastically): That's why we're here.

>   CORKY: What y'all think we do isn't exactly what happens in reality. And I'd like to explain.

INT. COLISEUM - LATE AFTERNOON
A U-Haul is admitted to a back entrance. Junior Wranglers frantically throw buckets upon buckets of snake remains into the U-Haul.

JSWs working the butchering area tear off their white, blood-stained coats and throw them into trash containers.

With high-pressure hoses, other JSWs wash blood and entrails down floor drains.

Chuck and another JSW carry big display boards out of a back room into the snake pit area. The boards explain the process of venom collection and the role venom plays in cancer research.

EXT. COLISEUM - LATE AFTERNOON

>CORKY: So, rattlesnakes are actually gainin' on us in population in certain areas. Like deer when they're takin' over your flower beds, eatin' all the daisies. We're just trying to control the species by huntin' selectively and humanely. Officer Pierce can tell you how we hunt the rattler—it's mighty civilized, ain't it, officer?

>ULYSSES: I found nothing objectionable.

>CORKY: There you go, eyewitness testimony.

>WOMAN PICKETER: We want to see inside.

>THE CROWD OF PICKETERS: Let us inside!

Toby gives Corky a nod.

>CORKY: Be my guest.

INT. COLISEUM - LATE AFTERNOON
With Corky still standing on the tail gate, the doors open, the pickup pulls forward and the crowd surges in. The Roundup has been reduced to one large pit, the display boards, and a few souvenirs. The coliseum is immaculate.

Rose and Ulysses enter.

>ROSE: Strange. I brought my fourth graders here on Friday, and there were several large kettles right there. And over there

was the butchering area. With buckets of rattlesnake heads.

> ULYSSES: I should have come here first thing. But Corky insisted on picking me up at the motel.

Corky enters the snake pit, where the snakes are sequestered in a small area. The snare-drum playing JSW is in the pit.

Corky walks to a table, where a microphone and a large graduated cylinder with a glass funnel sit. He picks up the microphone.

> CORKY: Ladies and gentlemen, may I have your attention, please.

A spotlight makes Suzie's Miss Snake Charmer banner sparkle as she descends the steps entering the pit, teetering on spike heels. She smiles and waves at the crowd.

INTERCUT - INT. VALJEAN'S APARTMENT - LATE AFTERNOON
Valjean bursts through the door and storms into the bedroom. He pulls two big suitcases out of the closet and starts throwing his clothes into them.

BACK TO SCENE

> CORKY: Last night our judges selected Miss Suzie Scrogie to be the new Miss Snake Charmer.

The Junior Snake Wranglers, and other Eden's Lair's townspeople, applaud enthusiastically.

Chuck reappears, sweaty and exhausted. He sees Suzie, smooths back his hair, and wipes his face and teeth with his shirt tail.

> CORKY: To provide y'all with a learnin' experience, she's agreed to give you a demonstration of how to milk a rattlesnake. And believe me, she's gonna have to use an awfully low stool.
>
> CHUCK (to himself): He uses that same joke every year.
>
> CORKY: Maestro?

The JSW begins to play his snare.

INTERCUT - INT. VALJEAN'S APARTMENT - LATE AFTERNOON
The mantle. Valjean removes his army photo, the childhood picture with Darlynn, and the one of his mother, and tosses them in a suitcase. He opens a desk drawer, removes a framed, autographed head shot of Corky, and hurls it at a wall.

BACK TO SCENE
Corky hands Suzie his snake hook and makes her pick up a snake sitting on a table.

> CORKY (quietly): Go easy. Don't worry about it, don't worry about it. Do just like I told you to do. Put your hook right behind his eyes. Move easy, move easy. Okay, pin him.
>
> SUZIE: Have I got him?

Suzie begins to slip the hook out from between her fingers and the back of the snake's head.

> CORKY: Remember them fangernails, remember them fangernails. He'd better cooperate, or he'll end up being somebody's belt.

INTERCUT - EXT. VALJEAN'S APARTMENT - LATE AFTERNOON

Valjean throws his suitcases in the back of the pickup. His M16 sits in the gun rack. He gets in the truck and speeds away.

BACK TO SCENE

Suzie slips the hook out.

> SUZIE: I got him!

> CORKY: Okay, lay your hook down and grab his body. Split his mouth on the funnel. Easy, easy!

The snake's fangs CLANG on the glass.

> CORKY: Now let go of his body; I got it. Feel his glands with your other hand. Work your way up, work it all the way up. Look, he's already started pumpin' it naturally.

INT./EXT. DARLYNN'S BEDROOM - DUSK

Darlynn stands at the open window looking out. To thwart her various escape attempts, Corky has wound barbed wire around the tree near the window. A strong gust of wind sweeps back her hair and breaks a large limb off the tree, taking a substantial portion of the barbed wire with it.

Darlynn goes to the closet and removes a set of chaps, a leather fringed jacket, a pair of leather gloves, and leather tennis shoes. She puts on this protective clothing and ties her hair back with a ribbon.

Gathering her courage, she climbs out the window.

EXT. THE HIGHWAY - DUSK
Valjean pulls over next to the "Eden's Lair, Texas, Rattlesnake Capital of the World" billboard and, with his M16, shoots out the word "Eden".

He drives into the coliseum parking lot. He spots Corky's truck and raises his rifle. He changes his mind—too many people in the parking lot. Too many witnesses. Too many innocents.

BACK TO SCENE
While flashes go off in her face, Suzie beams at the crowd.

> CORKY: Beauty and the beast, ladies and gentlemen, beauty and the beast. You wanna hug my neck?

> SUZIE: Yes, sir. Thank you.

Suzie hugs Corky. His hand traces the curve of her back.

> CORKY: Any time, any time.

Chuck presents Suzie with a bouquet of roses. She ascends the flight of steps attached to the side of the pit. Chuck helps her over.

Suzie bounces over to her mother and sister.

> SUZIE: Mom, Chucker here wants to take me out to dinner.

Suzie squeals.

> CHUCK: Compliments of the Roundup.

> PATTI: Okay, but don't keep her out too late.

> CHUCK: Don't worry, Mrs. Scrogie, she's in good hands.

Suzie adjusts her banner and takes Chuck's arm.

> MAN PICKETER (to Corky): What do you do with the venom?

> CORKY: Labs all over the world request it special. So if we stopped huntin' the rattler, we'd lose the war on cancer, and that would be doin' humanity a terrible disservice.

The picketers have mixed reactions.

> CORKY: Y'all step on over to our displays. They explain the whole process.

Corky leads a group of the activists over to the exhibits. Others start to trickle out of the coliseum. One even buys a rattlesnake hatband. Corky has satisfied their curiosity.

> ULYSSES (to Rose): I've seen enough, but the problem is, I haven't seen anything to shut them down. Think I'll head back

to the motel. Need a lift?

ROSE: Sure, thanks.

Corky leaves the group of activists and heads toward Ulysses and Rose. He stops by the souvenir table to collect two "Eden's Lair, Texas, Rattlesnake Capital of the World" ball caps and beer can "koozies," and two rolled-up pieces of parchment tied with ribbon.

CORKY: Y'all takin' off?

ULYSSES (handing Corky his keys): Yeah. I've got a big week ahead of me, and I'm sure Miss Rose does, too. Thanks for the use of your truck.

CORKY: And here's some souvenirs of our little Roundup. I'd like to present both of y'all with these suitable-for-framin' certificates that declare y'all Honorary Snake Wranglers, with all the privileges and entitlements that go along with it.

ULYSSES: Thanks for the special treatment, Mr. Dodds. We'll be in touch.

CORKY: Travel safe, and good night, Miss Rose. Pleasant dreams.

EXT. THE HIGHWAY - DUSK

An extraordinary sunset frames the plains as Ulysses and Rose drive down the highway. Huge thunderheads hang in the western sky.

They pass the caravan of lost activists, with Richard in the lead. Richard thinks he sees Rose and does a double take.

EXT. ROSE'S HOUSE - EVENING
Ulysses and Rose pull up in front of her house.

> ROSE: Thank you, Mr. Pierce. When are you heading back?
>
> ULYSSES: Probably within the hour. Gotta be at my desk bright and early. Not sure what happened to my colleagues from Lubbock?
>
> ROSE: Maybe they were thrown off the trail.
>
> ULYSSES: The sheriff's made himself scarce, too. I was hoping to speak with him before I left. Here's my card if you ever need to contact me.

Bluster is barking and throwing himself against the front door.

> ROSE: Have a safe trip back.

Ulysses watches to make sure Rose gets inside her home safely. She quickly opens the door, grabbing Bluster by the collar, turns and waves in his direction.

INT. ROSE'S KITCHEN - NIGHT
She bounds into the kitchen with Bluster at her heels and fixes his dinner.

She hears a tentative KNOCK on the door and grabs Bluster's collar.

ROSE: Mr. Pierce? Come on in, I'm holding Bluster.

A figure appears in the doorway. Rose turns around, expecting to see Mr. Pierce.

DARLYNN: Miss Rose?

Rose gasps.

DARLYNN: I'm Darlynn. Darlynn Dodds. Valjean's told me about you. I need somebody to talk to.

INT. KUNDOO'S CONVENIENCE STORE - NIGHT

Rose bursts through the door. Kundoo sees that Darlynn is outside in the car.

KUNDOO: Good evening, Miss Rose!

ROSE: Kundoo, I need to ask a favor. It's urgent.

Kundoo notices she is wearing the vial he gave her.

KUNDOO: I'm glad you didn't need to use that today. Everyone is talking about the snake-hunting schoolteacher. You are somewhat of a celebrity now.

Kundoo pulls out a revolver from a drawer under the counter and slides it toward Rose.

KUNDOO: You may need this.

ROSE: You read my mind. I'll return it in the morning.

KUNDOO: Please let me know if you see my little monkey. She disappeared late this afternoon.

ROSE (concerned): I will. Thank you!

EXT. MOTEL - NIGHT
Ulysses pulls into the parking space in front of his room. The Dallas activists' cars pull into the parking lot. They enter their rooms.

Richard is inside the motel office talking to the manager. The manager points to a location on a map; Richard folds up the map and leaves the office.

EXT. COLISEUM - NIGHT
Junior Snake Wranglers carry kegs of beer and huge slabs of barbecue into the coliseum.

Corky walks toward his truck, passing the chaps-wearing dancer escorted by two Junior Wranglers, one on each arm. The party's started.

DANCER: You ain't leavin', are you Corky?

CORKY: And miss the best part of Roundup weekend? I forgot somethin' in the truck, that's all. You wanna go find it with me?

DANCER: It's not some big ole snake, is it?

CORKY: It's big awright.

DANCER: It is slimy?

CORKY: Not yet.

The dancer laughs, and the threesome continues to the coliseum.

CORKY (under his breath, worried): I gotta find that goddamn boy of mine.

Corky sticks his hand in his pocket, pausing to adjust himself, and extracts his keys.

EXT. ROSE'S HOUSE - NIGHT
Richard exits his car. Bluster is barking, but when he sees Richard through the window, he starts leaping up and down and wagging his tail. Richard looks for a possible hidden key, but in vain.

INT. RESTAURANT - NIGHT
Iced tea slowly spins in Suzie's glass. Chuck pours a packet of sugar into his own iced tea and stirs it.

Suzie arrives at the table, sits down, and smells her hands.

SUZIE: I liked to never get that musty snake smell off.

CHUCK: Yeah, reminds me of somethin' else.

Chuck gives Suzie a sly look. They break into giggles.

CHUCK: A toast to the new Miss Snake Charmer.

They raise their glasses. Chuck slips the empty vial back into his pocket.

EXT./INT. DODD'S U-HAUL - NIGHT
Rose's car slowly pulls into the parking lot, headlights turned off. Darlynn exits the car, walks to a rock near the front door, and removes a key from under it. They enter the building.

> ROSE: Where's the key to the tornado shelter?

> DARLYNN: In Corky's desk drawer.

They leave the building, walk to the tornado shelter, unlock the padlock, and open the double doors.

INT. TORNADO SHELTER - NIGHT
They descend the steps.

> ROSE: Show me where, Darlynn. Don't be afraid.

Rose's flashlight illuminates a large room full of dusty boxes, old office furniture, and snake hunting equipment. The wind picks up outside, and the doors BANG on their hinges.

Darlynn leads Rose to a filing cabinet, locked, in the back of the shelter. She knows where the key is hidden, finds it, and unlocks the cabinet. It's full of scrapbooks of old newspaper clippings and photos. She sets them aside, carefully, revealing a false drawer. Darlynn hesitates, then removes the top. She lifts out a special scrapbook.

Darlynn hands it to Rose, steps back and covers her face. Rose opens the scrapbook.

EXT. TORNADO SHELTER - NIGHT
From inside the shelter, Darlynn emits a long, loud, primal SCREAM.

EXT. VALJEAN'S APARTMENT - NIGHT
Corky speeds past Valjean's apartment—his pickup isn't there.

EXT. DODD'S U-HAUL - NIGHT
Valjean's pickup is parked on a small rise near the U-Haul store. Corky speeds toward the store, and when he is a block away, BOOM! The truck spins out of control in loose gravel. Corky leaps out of his truck and examines the tire.

Gun raised, Valjean hesitates. Shooting a tire is one thing, but shooting his own father . . . He lowers his M16.

INT. TORNADO SHELTER - NIGHT
Hearing the gunshot and the blowout, Rose tucks the scrapbook under her arm, grabs Darlynn, and flies up the steps.

EXT./INT. DODD'S U-HAUL - NIGHT
Giant thunderheads RUMBLE as Rose and Darlynn leap into the car and speed away. Corky recognizes the car.

Corky runs into his store and sees the open desk drawer.

Valjean takes off in his pickup.

Corky looks out the window. The tornado shelter doors are open.

    CORKY: SHEE-YIT!

EXT./INT. MOTEL - NIGHT
Ulysses loads his bags into the trunk of the car. His cell phone rings inside the room and he misses the call. He returns to the room and sees that someone has left a message.

INT. DODD'S U-HAUL - NIGHT
Corky looks around for the keys to the one remaining U-Haul on the lot, a 26-footer. He finds them, runs outside, and speeds away.

EXT./INT. COLISEUM - NIGHT
Corky pulls into the parking lot in the U-Haul, barely missing several parked cars and drunk Junior Snake Wranglers.

He bursts through the front entrance and elbows his way through the throng of men. Beer sloshes onto his shirt from someone's mug.

In one of the pits, Jason has three snakes in each hand, in between his fingers.

> JASON: Look, Corky, a six-pack!

He twirls them around and around over his head like a lasso and then lets them go. They slam up against the wall.

EXT. MOTEL - NIGHT
Valjean swerves into the parking lot. Ulysses's car is gone.

INT. COLISEUM - NIGHT
In another pit, three Junior Snake Wranglers, including Adam, walk with their boots and spurs among coiled snakes, kicking them like hockey pucks into the wall. Corky walks past.

ADAM: Hey, Corky! The Kung-Fu death walk!

He pulls the outside corners of his eyelids up to look "Asian" and tries to kick a snake but misses and lands on his rear.

The woman wearing chaps performs for an eager audience.

Steve walks up to a cage sitting on a table. Bali the monkey is in the cage. Other Junior Snake Wranglers gather round. Steve opens the cage door and hands Bali a paper sack wrapped loosely with twine. He closes and locks the door.

Bali carefully removes the twine and looks inside the sack. Instead of finding a banana, he finds a rattlesnake. He begins to scream and run around the cage. The Junior Wranglers laugh and slap each other's backs and behinds.

The snake coils and strikes Bali, and Bali falls to the cage floor, dead.

Corky finds Steve.

STEVE: Where you been, Corky? You're missin' all the fun.

CORKY: Steve, Miss Rose is gettin' mighty nosey on us.

STEVE: You ain't scared of a little ole schoolteacher, are you?

CORKY: Naw, 'course I ain't.

STEVE: What's she up to?

CORKY: I got a pretty good idea, Steve, I got a pretty good idea. She'll be stoppin' by shortly.

STEVE: Seriously? This is the last place she'd come.

CORKY: You wait and see. It ain't gonna be good.

Rose and Darlynn pull into the parking area at the rear entrance. Rose takes a few deep breaths.

ROSE: Darlynn, honey, you stay here. Don't worry, I'll be back in a few minutes.

Large drops of rain descend to the pavement.

Rose sneaks into the coliseum through a back door and slips behind the bleachers. She watches what's going on from between the seats.

Chuck enters through the same back door with Suzie Scrogie, who can barely walk and is laughing. The drug Chuck slipped her at dinner has made her compliant and giddy.

Toby emerges from a back room and picks Suzie up in his arms. They disappear into the room.

Someone lays their hand on Rose's shoulder. She jumps.

VALJEAN: What are you doin' here?

ROSE: Now I know what "line-balled" means.

VALJEAN: We gotta go. Now.

ROSE: Not without Suzie. Is this what you wanted to tell me?

VALJEAN: I didn't know how. They won't be so nice with you, Rose. At least she won't remember it in the morning. (A beat) There's something else, Rose.

ROSE: I already know.

Valjean breaks down in sobs.

VALJEAN: Corky said he'd kill me if I told anyone. And he'd do it, too; he'd kill his own son. I hate myself for not protectin' Darlynn better.

Valjean is wearing his JSW vest and cowboy hat.

ROSE: Take off your vest. And give me your hat.

VALJEAN: It won't work. Think of yourself. Suzie'll be okay.

ROSE: I am thinking of myself.

Rose rips Valjean's vest off and snatches his hat.

ROSE: You should have told me.

VALJEAN: I was gonna tell you tonight at supper. And ask you to go away with me. Darlynn won't leave, but I got to.

Rose vanishes into the crowd.

INTERCUT - INT. RICHARD'S CAR - NIGHT
Richard speeds past the "Eden's Lair" billboard, that now reads "Lair, Texas, home of the World's Largest Rattlesnake Roundup".

>RICHARD: Rose. ROSE!!!

BACK TO SCENE
Rose reaches the closed door and hesitates. She pulls out the revolver.

Valjean pushes through an almost impenetrable crowd.

INT. BACK ROOM - NIGHT
Rose bursts through the door and sees a makeshift set for a photo shoot: a small snake pit, a table with coiled (taxidermied) rattle-snakes, a photomural backdrop of people sitting in the bleachers of a coliseum, and the giant papier-mâché rattlesnake that greets the public, normally placed at the entrance to the coliseum.

Toby grabs Rose.

Suzie is slumped in a chair, wearing chaps. Chuck has removed the Miss Snake Charmer banner and is unbuttoning her shirt. He turns to greet the intruder.

>CHUCK: Who's this?

Toby rips the revolver from her hand and yanks off her hat.

>CHUCK: Why, looky who's come to join the party! And she's packin'! This ain't no way for a nice little schoolteacher to act.

ROSE: I'm leaving with her, right now.

CHUCK: We ain't doin' nothin' to her that she ain't done before. Look, she ain't runnin' away, is she? She's a full-grown consentin' adult, fulfilling her duties as Miss Snake Charmer.

STEVE: She's charmin' my snake, that's for sure.

Suzie throws her head back and laughs.

ROSE: The sheriff's going to hear about this.

Chuck and Steve laugh.

CHUCK: You won't be tellin' him nothin' he don't already know.

Steve stands guard at the door.

STEVE: You know the rules. Any woman who comes into the coliseum during our little party is fair game. And they know better than to talk about it afterwards.

INTERCUT - DALLAS STREET - NIGHT
POV Rose, SCREAMING. Her assailant covers her mouth and drags her into an alley. Two accomplices run into the alley after them.

BACK TO SCENE
The door bursts open, almost sending Steve crashing to the floor. It's Corky, with a camera swinging from his shoulder.

CORKY: Boys, we're gonna have to finish up here pretty quick.

Corky gets right up into Rose's face.

CORKY: There's a snake in your bed. It's long and hard and wants to crawl up inside you.

A snake hook lands hard on Corky's back. He manages to turn around and face his assailant before collapsing. It's Valjean.

Toby releases Rose to help Corky, and Valjean plants his fist in Chuck's stomach.

Rose and Valjean grab Suzie.

VALJEAN: Let's go!

INT. COLISEUM - NIGHT
Rose and Valjean drag Suzie through the crowd. Corky catches up with them. He spins Valjean around.

They are no longer father and son; they are bitter enemies. Corky strikes the first blow.

The Junior Snake Wranglers gather in a circle around them. The distraction allows Rose to escape with Suzie.

They run into Earl Scrogie, her father.

EARL: Suzie! What are you doing here?

Suzie shrugs her shoulders and laughs.

ROSE: Leave! Get her out of here!

Corky taunts Valjean.

CORKY: Valjean, I swear you can't get no dummer. Anything happens to me's gonna happen to you, too.

VALJEAN: No, it ain't, Corky. I ain't got nothin' to do with you no more.

CORKY: Like hell!

The coliseum doors fly open. A wall of rain is sucked inside. Four Texas Rangers trucks, their lights flashing, block the entrance.

Wielding a megaphone, Ulysses appears, flanked by the Lubbock Rangers.

ULYSSES: Everybody freeze. The party's over, snake motherfuckers!

CORKY: I never did think nothin' of you, boy.

VALJEAN: You sick, filthy bastard!

Valjean knocks Corky out cold and disappears into the crowd. Chaos erupts.

Toby and Steve pursue Rose as she tries to escape. They catch up to her without much difficulty.

STEVE: Here's what you git for bustin' up our little party.

Toby picks up Rose and tosses her into the snake pit. The snakes are aggressive and angry. One approaches Rose and coils to strike. She resists the urge to flee. The snake sinks its fangs deep into her thigh.

She feels for Kundoo's vial, fishes it out from underneath her blouse, and it's broken. A few precious drops cling to its ragged edge, which she places on her tongue before passing out.

EXT. COLISEUM - NIGHT
Richard pulls into the parking lot amid the chaos. He bursts out of the car and approaches a Texas RANGER.

> RICHARD: Do you know if Rose McGrath is in there?

> RANGER: She's the teacher who busted up the Roundup, right? It's likely.

INT. COLISEUM - NIGHT
Ulysses sees Rose and calls for an ambulance on his radio. Richard arrives at the pit and, horror-stricken, scrambles into the pit, gently lifts her, and carries her out.

The wind outside has picked up considerably. The sides of the coliseum vibrate and groan. Golf-ball-sized hail begins to fall.

EXT. COLISEUM - NIGHT
A crush of people streams out of the coliseum and head for their cars.

Richard carefully places Rose onto a gurney. He and the AMBULANCE DRIVER put her into the back of the ambulance.

Richard climbs inside and sits beside her.

    RICHARD: Rose, it's me. I'm here. Hold on.

Still sitting in Rose's car, in the back of the coliseum, Darlynn watches in horror as the building sways in the wind and people continue to stream out.

Valjean staggers out of the coliseum. Darlynn sees him, opens the car door, and jumps out.

    DARLYNN: Valjean!!

Suddenly, the rain stops, and everything is still.

The townspeople pause to listen. Valjean stops dead in his tracks.

A sound in the distance, like a TRAIN, is coming closer.

Mass confusion erupts. A tornado is approaching.

Cars and trucks smash into each other as people try to get out of the parking lot. The train sound grows louder and louder.

The ambulance is out on the road when an explosion launches debris in all directions—the tornado has collided with the coliseum.

INT. AMBULANCE - NIGHT
Rose is not responsive.

BEGIN DREAM SEQUENCE
Rose lies unconscious on her kitchen floor surrounded by hundreds of snakes. Kundoo's voice awakens her.

> KUNDOO (V.O.): Miss Rose, stand up. Stand up and walk to the door.

With the same motion as Kundoo's pet cobra, her body becomes vertical. Her legs are bound tightly by several snakes.

> ROSE: I. Can't. Move.

> KUNDOO: You must get to the door, quickly!

Slowly, she glides to the door and pushes it open. The house is teetering at the edge of a raging river.

The wooden raft floats up to her. Lying on it is a pole. The snakes loosen their grip and slither into the water. She leaps onto the raft, grabs the pole, and starts to push. It has absolutely no effect, but as the raft hurtles down-river, she grabs a tree limb and pulls herself to the opposite short.

EXT. HIGHWAY - NIGHT
Valjean and Darlynn speed down the highway in his truck, dodging debris. Telephone wires swing from their poles like children's jump ropes.

A telephone pole uproots and becomes airborne. It lands horizontally on the roof of a car up ahead. The driver loses control of the car and smashes into another telephone pole.

Valjean and Darlynn pull up behind the car and leap out. Valjean rolls the pole off the car onto the ground. Through what used to be the windshield, he looks at the driver.

> VALJEAN: Kundoo!

Kundoo is fatally injured.

> KUNDOO: Miss Rose. The hospital. Quickly!

Kundoo hands Valjean his necklace with the vial.

> VALJEAN: Hold on, Kundoo, I'll send help!

EXT. HOSPITAL - NIGHT
The ambulance with Rose and Richard pulls up to the ER entrance. The driver leaps out and flings open the doors.

Rose has an eerie look on her swollen face. Richard is crying and stroking her hair.

Dr. Ennis rushes out to greet the ambulance.

> DR. ENNIS: Get her to the ER, NOW! (to himself) Lord, I haven't had to treat a real one of these in years.

INT. HOSPITAL CORRIDOR/OPERATING ROOM - NIGHT
Two ORDERLIES wheel Rose down a corridor with a NURSE following alongside. Valjean and Darlynn burst through a door and follow. The nurse unbuttons the cuffs on Rose's long-sleeved shirt and rolls up her sleeves.

Valjean sees two ugly, pink scars that traverse her wrists.

> ORDERLY: Back off, Valjean. Ain't you never seen a suicide attempt before?

The orderly pushes Valjean out of the way, rolls the gurney into the operating room, and shuts the door on Valjean and Darlynn. The nurse starts hooking Rose up to monitors.

Richard and Dr. Ennis enter the room. Valjean and Darlynn walk in after them. Darlynn retreats to a dark corner of the room.

> NURSE: 70 over 40, Doctor.

> DR. ENNIS (to Richard): I don't suppose you know if she's allergic to antivenin?

> RICHARD: It's never come up.

> DR. ENNIS (to the nurse): Well, I guess we'll find out. Six vials to start.

CONTINUE DREAM SEQUENCE
As Rose pulls herself closer to the tree, the waters recede. It is the large oak tree in Eden's Lair's town square. A huge, thick serpent is twined around its trunk. She steps on its tail accidentally and arouses him.

Slowly, she backs away from the serpent. Acorns on the tree begin to grow into luscious, ripe apples. The Eden's Lair's mothers with their baby strollers appear and sit on park benches across from the tree.

Darlynn materializes, sitting at the base of the tree next to the snake.

>   DARLYNN: The snake enticed me, and so I ate.

Several babies float out of their carriages and over to the tree. The babies circle round the tree like electrons in their orbits around a nucleus. The huge snake strikes at the babies, killing them one-by-one. Darlynn runs away. The mothers are indifferent.

The snake begins twisting the tree back and forth, causing the limbs to shake violently. Apples fall to the ground.

A large sword appears and challenges the snake. Rose is drawn irrevocably to the tree. The sword strikes at her; she ducks and backs off.

With its head, the snake pushes one of the apples in her direction and it rolls to her feet. The sword "sees" what he has done and swiftly chops off its head.

Rose picks up the apple and studies its shiny surface and perfect form. She sees her ashen face reflected in its skin.

BACK TO SCENE

>   NURSE: Doctor, her platelets are not improving. No control has been established.

>   DR. ENNIS: Okay, administer another six vials while I check for internal bleeding. (to himself) Good Lord!

CONTINUE DREAM SEQUENCE
Rose's reflection in the apple starts to vibrate. A very deep RUMBLE boils up from the center of the Earth. In the distance, a huge, black tornado ejects what look like pieces of doll houses from its funnel.

Kundoo descents from the clouds, wearing white, flowing robes, and opens his robes to reveal the Dallas crime scene, as seen from above.

We see the street, Rose walking down the street to her car, her assailant grabbing her and dragging her in the alley, and his two accomplices following behind.

Richard runs into the frame and enters the alley.

The POV changes to street level, and we see Richard desperately and valiantly fighting off all three men, but he is no match for their strength and numbers.

BACK TO SCENE
Rose's face and throat swell. Blood dribbles from the corners of her mouth.

Valjean approaches Richard.

> VALJEAN: Who the hell are you?

> DR. ENNIS (to Valjean): Stop, please! (to Richard) She's bleeding internally. What type are you?

> RICHARD: A-minus.

DR. ENNIS: Valjean?

VALJEAN: O-positive. The best blood there is.

DR. ENNIS: Nurse, run a pre-transfusion test.

CONTINUE DREAM SEQUENCE
A desolate prairie near Eden's Lair. Rose's standing body is entangled in a huge snake. Kundoo walks into the frame.

KUNDOO: Those who love you are here. Let them help!

Richard appears and tries to pry the snake loose from Rose. The snake strikes at him repeatedly, but Richard is not to be deterred. The snake entwines them both tightly together, spiraling up their bodies. When its face reaches their faces, its body splits and turns into a huge hawk. The hawk hovers over Kundoo, flapping its powerful wings. It grabs Kundoo by the shoulders, and they vanish into the sky. The tornado follows. All is still.

BACK TO SCENE
Valjean's blood is transfusing into Rose as he monitors her face, watching for a change in expression. Richard holds her hand, absentmindedly stroking the scar on her wrist. The vital signs monitor flat lines.

DR. ENNIS: Nurse, the AED, now!

More equipment is wheeled into place. Dr. Ennis opens the front of her blouse and begins prepping Rose for defibrillation. The nurse removes Valjean's and Rose's needles and places gauze and Band-Aids on the wounds. Valjean sees the necklace with the vial and realizes it's identical to his.

VALJEAN: Oh my God!

He produces the necklace given to him by Kundoo, unscrews the top of the vial, and gently lifts Rose's head off the pillow.

RICHARD: Hold on there! Take your hands off my wife.

VALJEAN: Open her mouth!

RICHARD (to Dr. Ennis): Who is this guy?

A long beat. The room is silent, except for the sound of the vital signs monitor, still flat-lined. Rose remains unresponsive.

VALJEAN: DOCTOR ENNIS!

DR. ENNIS: Let him do it.

The nurse opens Rose's mouth while Valjean pours in the contents of the vial. He tilts her head back. Some of it runs down her cheek. Nothing happens.

Another long beat. Dr. Ennis initiates the AED machine. Suddenly, with a loud gasp, Rose opens her eyes.

RICHARD: Rose!

She dabs at her mouth, looks at her hands, and is horrified to see the blood on her swollen fingers.

VALJEAN: Thank God!

ROSE: Richard! I should be surprised to see you, but somehow, I'm not.

RICHARD: I'm here for you, Rose.

She lifts her necklace and sees the broken vial.

ROSE: Kundoo's potion.

Valjean holds his up for her to see.

VALJEAN: He gave me one, too.

Rose remembers her dream.

ROSE: I saw Kundoo.

The nurse raises the head of the bed.

ROSE (to Richard): He showed me how you tried to save me. He told me I would make it. (to Valjean) And that those who love me would help.

She sees the Band-Aids covering the wounds in Valjean's arm and in hers. A beatific expression floods her face, and the swelling vanishes.

Tears well up in Valjean's eyes and begin to roll down his cheeks. Overcome, he runs from the room.

Ulysses enters dragging Corky by his hand cuffs. Corky has a black eye and a deep gash across his forehead. He flashes an icy stare at Rose.

> ULYSSES (to Rose): I thought you'd like to see the result of your handiwork, Miss Rose.

Corky notices Darlynn standing in the corner.

> CORKY: I just saw your brother runnin' away like the coward he is. And what the hell are you doin' here?

Darlynn steps out into the light.

> DARLYNN: For years I thought that bein' with you was my duty. Then I was just plain afraid to stop. You made me feel like I was the lowest thing in the world, but now I know better. Miss Rose says I don't have to let you do that to me no more.

> CORKY: You're a liar and a whore!

> DARLYNN: I used to believe you, but I don't no more. I used to respect you, too, but I don't no more neither. And I never, ever, want to see your face again. Never!

Darlynn runs from the room.

> ULYSSES: Well, Rose, that (he's searching for words) document will keep ole Corky Dodds out of commission for a long time. And with the coliseum gone, I don't think there'll be much of a roundup from now on, either.

CORKY: Miss Rose, I want you to think about somethin'. What you did has destroyed a family and the whole town of Eden's Lair, too. We don't have no identity without the Roundup. And let me tell you somethin' else. You have challenged the word of God almighty hisself. God cursed the serpent, and God cursed woman. And don't you forget that. I was just witnessin' for the Lord, that's all I was doin'.

ROSE (to Richard): I'd like to give us another chance. Let's go home.

EXT. TOWN SQUARE - EARLY MORNING
Debris lies all around the huge oak tree, which was untouched by the tornado. Its limbs are draped with the bodies of snakes. A hawk perches in its upper limbs.

A fire hydrant shoots a stream of water into the street. Votive offerings that had been placed on the tree float on the water and disappear into a sewer.

The Junior Snake Wranglers and their wives clean up glass and debris in front of their businesses. Disoriented dogs run through the streets.

EXT. ESCARPMENT - EARLY MORNING
Valjean's truck is parked on its edge. He sits on the hood looking down at the destruction. Eden's Lair doesn't look like Hollywood anymore.

Darlynn joins him. Their eyes meet, and Darlynn smiles for the first time. It's a beautiful, radiant smile.

Valjean walks around to the back of the pickup and secures their luggage.

Brother and sister drive away.

Back to the view of the escarpment. A lustrous sunrise bathes the town of Eden's Lair in golden light. The hawk flies past and into the distance until he disappears from sight.

THE END

ABOUT THE AUTHOR

Strake Colton has written three screenplays, two book-length works of fiction, poetry, and short stories. Originally from Dallas, Texas, he now lives in Santa Fe, New Mexico.